Training Circular
No. 7-101

TC 7-101
Headquarters
Department of the Army
Washington, DC, 26 November 2010

Exercise Design

Contents

Distribution Restriction: Approved for public release; distribution is unlimited.

Figures

Tables

Preface

This training circular (TC) outlines a methodology for designing and executing training exercises. It describes planning procedures and methodologies, responsibilities, and analysis for those who plan and control Army exercises intended as culminating collective training events that critically assess unit-training status. Collective training is part of unit training. It is performance oriented and a command responsibility executed by leaders at all echelons. As a continuous process executed in accordance with a formal training program, collective training trains units and teams on tasks and missions they are expected to perform. It is executed in a crawl-walk-run approach and reaches across all training domains and integrated live, virtual, constructive, and gaming training environments.

This publication applies to the Active Army, the Army National Guard (ARNG)/Army National Guard of the United States (ARNGUS), and the United States Army Reserve (USAR) unless otherwise stated.

Headquarters, U.S. Army Training and Doctrine Command (TRADOC) is the proponent for this TC. The preparing agency is the Contemporary Operational Environment and Threat Integration Directorate (CTID), TRADOC G-2 Intelligence Support Activity (TRISA)–Threats. Send comments and suggested improvements on DA Form 2028 (Recommended Changes to Publications and Blank Forms) directly to CTID at the following address: Director, CTID, TRADOC G-2 Intelligence Support Activity–Threats, ATTN: ATIN-T (Bldg 53), 700 Scott Avenue, Fort Leavenworth, KS 66027-1323. This publication is available at Army Knowledge Online (AKO) at http://www.us.army.mil and the Reimer Digital Library at http://www.train.army.mil.

Readers should monitor those sites and also the TRADOC G2-TRISA Website at: https://www.us.army.mil/suite/files/14705412 (AKO access required) for the status of this TC and information regarding updates. Periodic updates, subject to the normal approval process, will occur as a result of the normal production cycle. The date on the cover and title page of the electronic version will reflect the latest update.

This page intentionally left blank.

Introduction

This training circular (TC) outlines a methodology for designing and executing training exercises. It describes planning procedures and methodologies, responsibilities, and analysis for those who plan and control Army exercises intended as culminating collective training events that critically assess unit-training status. The objective of exercise design is to structure a training event that establishes the conditions to facilitate performance-oriented training on properly selected, directed, and mission essential training objectives.

The references section of this TC contains a listing of publications pertaining and relating to this publication. The glossary contains abbreviations and special terms used in this TC.

This TC is a planning and design tool that significantly enhances an exercise planner's ability to produce an operational environment (OE) that achieves desired unit training objectives while fielding a challenging opposing force (OPFOR) consistent with Hybrid Threat OPFOR doctrine as described in the TC 7-100 series. This TC provides the exercise planner with a backbone methodology for scenario development and establishment of the exercise OE. The approach to exercise design and analysis is sequential and structured to get the planner to the "bottom-line" as quickly as possible.

Figure 1 shows the tools necessary and available for the design of a training exercise. While the process is sequential, many of the steps and procedures are developed concurrently and may overlap (see chapter 2). This TC is meant to be used in conjunction with the 7-100 series as well as the other publications listed in figure 1. These tools can be found at https://www.us.army mil/suite/files/14705412. Together, these tools outline an OPFOR than can cover the full spectrum of military and paramilitary capabilities against which the Army must train to ensure success in the types of OEs it can expect to encounter now and in the clearly foreseeable future.

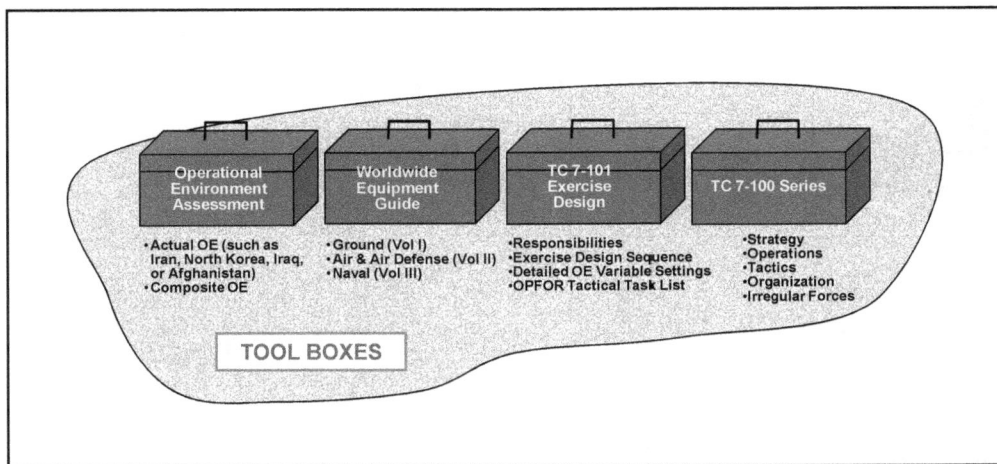

Figure 1. Exercise design tools

The processes described in this TC are applicable to any number of exercise venues to include field training exercises, command post exercises, and simulations. They can also be used in the development of mission rehearsal exercises (MRXs). The operational variables (political, military, economic, social, information, infrastructure, physical environment, and time [PMESII-PT]) and the settings for their subvariables, as described in chapter 3, can be used to develop OEs for exercises or for describing actual OEs portrayed in MRXs.

Each chapter of the TC covers a specific aspect of exercise design. The exercise planner should become familiar with each chapter.

In order to train against a realistic threat and in a realistic OE, the OE must be dynamic. By using the PMESII-PT variables and incorporating them into every aspect of the scenario, the training unit will experience a realistic and challenging exercise every time. This TC describes the roles and responsibilities of the senior trainer, exercise director, and exercise planner; the importance of quality training objectives, the steps to designing an exercise; and the theory behind exercise design. The bottom line is that this TC gives planners the tools to provide the correct exercise conditions for the training unit's training objectives, resulting in effective training.

Chapter 1

Responsibilities

This chapter establishes the responsibilities for exercise development. The senior trainer, the exercise director and the exercise planner are the individuals primarily responsible for exercise development and execution. Table 1-1 provides an example of how a unit can determine who will be the senior trainer, exercise director, and exercise planner for various levels of organizations.

Table 1-1. Example guide to determine roles

	Training Unit	Senior Trainer	Exercise Director	Exercise Planner
Joint Training Exercise	Division	Corps Cdr	J7	J7 Ops
CTC Training Exercise	Brigade	Division Cdr	Combat Training Center CG	COG/Ops
Active Component Home Station Training Exercise	Battalion	Brigade Cdr	Division G3	G3 Training
Reserve Component Home Station Training Exercise	Battalion	Brigade Cdr	Training Support Battalion Cdr	G3 Training

1-1.   The senior trainer is the commander of the parent organization of the unit being trained. This commander has two major overall training responsibilities: develop Soldiers and leaders for future responsibilities and prepare his unit to accomplish the assigned mission. In the absence of a directed mission, commanders must prepare their unit to perform those core missions the unit was doctrinally designed to execute across the full range of military operations.

1-2.   The senior trainer conducts the first, and most important, step in creating the tools necessary for exercise design. He determines the exact troop list for the training unit. When establishing the troop list, the senior trainer should—

- Identify the task organization of the unit to be trained.
  - Complete task-organizing, to include types and numbers of equipment.
  - Ideally, training level and maintenance history should be included.
- Identify key echelons to be trained.
  - Multi-echelon training leaves many out of training if not planned for early.
- Lock in troop list early.
  - Late changes may require a scenario rewrite and should not be just pasted into the original scenario.

1-3.   The senior trainer determines the training objectives of the exercise. Training objectives are described in chapter 2. The senior trainer ensures the unit's training objectives support the approved mission essential task list (METL). (See chapter 2.) After mission essential tasks are selected, the senior trainer identifies supporting training objectives for each task. According to FM 7-0, each training objective has three parts:

- **Task.** A clearly defined and measurable activity accomplished by individuals and organizations. Tasks are specific activities that contribute to the accomplishment of encompassing missions or other requirements.
- **Condition(s).** Those variables of an operational environment or situation in which a unit, system, or individual is expected to operate and may affect performance. (JP 1-02)
- **Standard.** A quantitative or qualitative measure and criterion for specifying the levels of performance of a task. (FM 7-0)

1-4. The senior trainer ensures the unit refers to the applicable documents to identify the conditions and standards for its essential tasks. The documents listed in figure 1-1 will assist units in developing collective and individual training objectives.

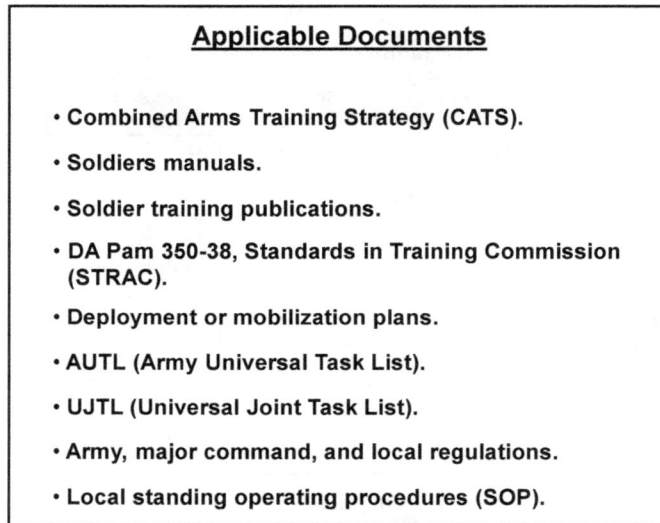

Applicable Documents

- **Combined Arms Training Strategy (CATS).**

- **Soldiers manuals.**

- **Soldier training publications.**

- **DA Pam 350-38, Standards in Training Commission (STRAC).**

- **Deployment or mobilization plans.**

- **AUTL (Army Universal Task List).**

- **UJTL (Universal Joint Task List).**

- **Army, major command, and local regulations.**

- **Local standing operating procedures (SOP).**

Figure 1-1. Training objective development sources

1-5. The senior trainer, in conjunction with the commander of the unit to be trained, conducts an assessment of the current training state of the unit immediately prior to the exercise. This anticipated training condition of the unit, as it enters the exercise, is expressed as trained (T), partially trained (P), or untrained (U). (See FM 7-0.)

1-6. The senior trainer, along with the commander of the training unit, must bring the following tools to the initial planning: the troop list, the proposed training objectives (METL), the proposed conditions for the training objective tasks, and the commander's assessment. (See figure 1-2.) During the analysis of these tools, discussion and negotiations of the initial planning phase, the senior trainer will issue guidance.

```
                        Mission Essential Task:

                           Conduct an Attack

                           Conditions:

The brigade is conducting operations independently or as part of a division or Army forces (ARFOR) and has
received an operation order (OPORD) or fragmentary order (FRAGO) to conduct an attack at the location
and time specified. Coalition forces and noncombatants may be present in the operational environment.

                           Standards:

1.  Brigade leaders gain and or maintain situational awareness. Brigade commander and staff receive an
    order or anticipate a new mission and begin the military decision making process. Brigade task
    organizes forces within the brigade.
2.  Effects coordination cell obtains guidance from the commander; plans, coordinates, and achieves the
    desired effects utilizing organic and attached assets.
3.  Staff plans mobility, countermobility, and survivability; nuclear, biological, and chemical support; air
    defense support; and CSS operations.
4.  Brigade commander and staff conduct risk management process.
5.  Brigade commander and staff conduct backbriefs and rehearsals to ensure subordinates understand
    commander's intent and concept.
6.  Brigade executes the attack; masses all available combat power to destroy enemy per the
    commander's intent.
7.  Brigade consolidates and reorganizes as necessary.
8.  Brigade continues operations as necessary.
```

Figure 1-2. Example of a brigade commander's training objective for his METL attack task

1-7. The exercise director is an officer of at least equal but preferred to be one grade higher than the senior trainer and is not part of the tactical chain of command of the training unit. However, during single-service Army exercises conducted largely with unit internal resources and not intended to be a culminating training event, the exercise director and senior trainer may be the same officer.

1-8. The exercise director—
- Creates and enforces the essential conditions called for by the training objectives. He is ultimately responsible for approving the combination of settings for the operational variables selected by the exercise planner.
- Ensures an effective training environment to create the most realistic training. He emplaces a strong safety program and develops and coordinates training events that synchronize training areas and facilities, training support systems products and services, opposing force (OPFOR), observer/controllers, evaluators, and all other resources to support the required conditions. Figure 1-3 on page 1-4 shows training events the exercise director will typically develop.
- Acts as honest broker and ensures a level playing field. The exercise director enforces use of OPFOR doctrine and exercise rules of engagement (EXROE). The exercise director achieves these primarily through a well-trained and properly resourced observer/controller organization.

• Joint Training Exercise	• Combined Training Exercise
• Situational Training Exercise	• Tactical Exercise Without Troops
• Command Field Exercises	• Deployment Exercise
• Logistic Exercise	• Combined Arms Live Fire Exercise
• Live Fire Exercise	• Field Training Exercise
• Map Exercise	• Fire Coordination Exercise
• CTC Rotations	• Battle Command Training Program
• Mission Rehearsal Exercise	Warfighter Exercise

Figure 1-3. Training events the exercise director will typically develop

1-9. The exercise planner is typically an officer tasked with the actual creation of the exercise and its conditions. He incorporates the training objectives, desired training conditions, resources available, commander's evaluation, and guidance from the exercise director into a cohesive exercise design. The exercise planner will—

- Develop the exercise scenario. Using exercise parameters as discussed in chapter 2, and the methodologies outlined in this TC, the exercise planner develops reasonable courses of action for both the training unit and OPFOR consistent with the TC 7-100 series and the selected operational environment (OE). However, if the training event is an MRX, the OPFOR should have maximum fidelity to a known enemy force in the actual OE for which the training unit is being prepared for deployment. Regardless of the type of training event, the planner builds an exercise framework, which contains the critical facts and conditions for the exercise. The exercise planner must keep in mind that, although the sequence of events that lead to the execution of a mission during training may be scripted and controlled, once the conditions for the mission are met and the unit begins mission execution, the events should be allowed to move along their natural course. He ensures that there is the least possible restraint on exercise conditions consistent with the training objectives that will allow leaders to realize the full consequences of their decisions.

- Determine the settings for the operational variables (political, military, economic, social, information, infrastructure, physical environment and time [PMESII-PT]), establishing a framework to build a dynamic and realistic OE. (See chapters 2 and 3.)

- Develop all orders, plans and instructions associated with the exercise to include the road to war, the training unit's orders and plans (parent unit and higher), OPFOR combat instructions (orders), and role-player instructions. During MRXs, the exercise planner may be responsible for development and coordination of controlled scripted events normally executed by OPFOR and other role-players.

- Develop concept briefings and interim progress reports and coordinate all aspects of the exercise closely with the exercise director to ensure compliance with guidance, support of the exercise training objectives and adherence to OPFOR doctrine.

- Exercise caution when using material from prior exercises. This TC was developed specifically to provide the exercise planner the outline and basic planning considerations necessary to develop coherent and meaningful training exercises based on the Contemporary Operational Environment (COE). Often, when given the assignment to design an exercise, an exercise planner will dust off a prior exercise and use it without modification. This is common practice and is common sense to use the prior work of those who came before instead of starting from nothing. If using a prior exercise, the exercise planner must view it only as an initial guide and, more importantly, still go through all the steps and use the after action review (AAR) from the prior exercise to prevent repetition of poorly planned or executed scenarios and events.

Chapter 2

Exercise Design Sequence

There are four phases the exercise planner goes through to develop a collective training event that critically assesses unit training status at any level. The exercise design sequence takes the exercise planner from the initial determination of exercise parameters, through countertask and operational environment (OE) development, and concludes with orders production.

2-1.   During phase 1 (initial planning), the training unit and the exercise director determine the exercise parameters to start the design process. Once the design parameters and prioritized training objectives are determined, the focus in phase 2 (task and countertask development) is on developing opposing force (OPFOR) tasks that counter the training unit's training objectives. Once phase 2 is completed, the exercise planner has the necessary tools to create the conditions of the OE in phase 3, (PMESII-PT OE development). Finally, during phase 4 (orders, plans, and instruction development), the exercise planner produces the orders, plans, and instructions that translate the OE decisions that were made in phase 3 into the products necessary for the training unit to conduct the exercise. Table 2-1 shows the exercise design sequence. It lists who should be involved in each phase, what tools are required, what key decisions must be made, and what the final products of the phase will be. **Essential to all phases is the understanding of the concept of an OE and all the associated operational variables that affect military operations and training.** Chapter 3 will describe, in detail, each operational variable and its subvariables.

Table 2-1. Exercise design sequence

Exercise Design Sequence	Phase 1 Initial Planning	Phase 2 Task and Countertask Development	Phase 3 PMESII-PT OE Development	Phase 4 Orders, Plans, and Instruction Development
WHO:	• Training Unit Commander • Exercise Director • Exercise Planner • Senior Trainer	• Exercise Planner • OPFOR Commander	• Exercise Planner	• Exercise Planner • Exercise Director
TOOLS:	• Troop List • Proposed Training Objectives • AUTL/UJTL • Requested Conditions • Commander's Training Assessment • Exercise Resources • Exercise Director's Initial Guidance	• Defined Exercise Parameters • Prioritized Training Objectives (METL) • TC 7-100 Series • OPFOR Tactical Task List • Worldwide Equipment Guide (WEG)*	• OE Assessment (OEA) • PMESII-PT Subvariables • Prioritized Training Objectives (METL) • OPFOR Countertasks • OE/WFF Analysis Matrix	• Defined OE • TC 7-100 Series • COA Sketch • OPFOR OB
KEY DECISIONS:	• Exercise Timeline • Type of Exercise • Operational Theme • Existing OEA or Composite OE	• Training Unit Tasks • OPFOR Countertasks • OPFOR OB* • OPFOR Task Organization* • OPFOR Tier Levels*	• PMESII-PT Subvariable Selection • Common Processes • Key Events	• Chronology of Key Events • C-,M- and D-Day • STARTEX • Disposition of Forces
PRODUCTS:	• Defined Exercise Parameters • Prioritized Training Objectives (METL)	• Developed Tasks and Countertasks • OPFOR OB* • OPFOR Task Organization* • OPFOR Tier Levels*	• OE/WFF Analysis • Refined Training Objectives and Task Organization • Developed OE	• Higher Unit OPLANs and Orders • OPFOR Orders • ROE • Role-Player Instructions • Road to War

* Phase 2 is the earliest point at which OPFOR OB and task organization, along with adjustment of OPFOR equipment tiers (using the WEG), could occur. However, this could also begin or be refined in phase 3 or phase 4.

SECTION I - PHASE 1: INITIAL PLANNING

2-2.   The initial step in the exercise design process is the most critical. The senior trainer, exercise director, and exercise planner meet for the first time at an initial planning conference to conduct preliminary planning and establish the parameters for the exercise. In many areas of the exercise, there is great uncertainty as to whether a new design will actually do what is desired, and new scenarios often have unexpected problems. The purpose of initial planning is to define and develop the parameters of the exercise. By defining the exercise parameters, certain key decisions can be made, which gives the exercise planner the tools necessary to begin developing the exercise. The initial planning establishes who is to be trained, where they are to be trained, expected training outcomes, and what broad conditions will be replicated in the exercise's OE to meet the training objectives.

TOOLS

2-3.   The training unit's commander, the exercise director, and the exercise planner must be present at phase 1 for initial planning. During the initial planning phase, the training unit commander must provide the exercise director and exercise planners with the following parameters:

- Troop list of unit to be trained.
- Proposed training objectives based on HQDA-approved mission essential task list (METL).
- Unit-requested conditions.
- Available exercise resources (such as training area, support, simulations).
- Commander's assessment of the unit's current training status.

2-4.   The training unit troop list should identify as closely as possible the actual task organization, number of Soldiers of the units participating in the exercise, and their equipment. The exercise planner needs to identify the key echelons to be trained and lock in the troop list as early as possible in the exercise development process to avoid time-consuming scenario rewrites. Additionally, a list of key leaders, their experience level, recent training, and time in position is helpful in gauging command and staff experience, which may influence training conditions and operational tempo (OPTEMPO).

2-5.   Developed from established unit METLs, training objectives represent focal points for the exercise planner when developing courses of action (COAs) and the supporting OE. The accomplishment of the training objectives is the prime reason exercises are conducted. Training objectives are statements that describe the desired outcome of a training activity in the unit (FM 7-0). They consist of tasks, conditions, and standards. The development of training objectives is fully discussed in FM 7-15.

2-6.   Some training environments are pre-determined based on the use of "live" training sites such as the maneuver combat training centers (MCTCs) or because units are training for specific situations in specific places (that is, mission rehearsal exercises). However, units participating in simulations or command post exercises (CPXs) may ask that a specific venue be developed to support the units training. The training unit may also request specific conditions in which to perform tasks.

2-7.   Resources to be considered by the exercise planner include—

- The amount of time available to complete the training.
- Support personnel required.
- Simulations available.
- Observer-controller support.
- OPFOR augmentation.
- Transportation assets.
- Available training areas.
- Training facilities.

The amount of available resources can limit the size or number of live training events (for example, field training and live fire exercises), requiring commanders to substitute a mix of virtual and constructive simulation exercises.

2-8. As discussed in chapter 1, the senior trainer, in conjunction with the commander of the unit to be trained, conducts an assessment of the anticipated training status of the training unit immediately prior to the exercise. This training condition of the unit as it enters the exercise is expressed as T-P-U (trained, needs practice, and untrained) in accordance with FM 7-0. This status provides the exercise planner and/or OPFOR commander critical information on the proper mix of OPFOR units and other conditions needed for the exercise.

2-9. It is essential that the exercise director is involved throughout the entire exercise planning process and especially during phase 1. If the exercise director is not involved with the initial key decisions that are made to design the framework of the exercise, problems may evolve later when the exercise director arrives and the exercise is not going as he envisioned. The exercise director must provide initial guidance and also broker the compromises that must often be made in the decisions concerning the proper training objectives to train toward. Often the available resources are not available to meet all the desired training objectives and conditions. Therefore, a decision must be made as to what risk is acceptable in limiting the number of objectives, which can then reduce the level of fidelity of the OE conditions.

KEY DECISIONS

2-10. Several key decisions need to be made at this point:
- What are the time parameters of the exercise?
- Will the exercise be live, virtual, constructive, gaming, or a combination?
- What is the operational theme?
- Will the scenario be based on an existing operational environment assessment (OEA) for an actual OE or a composite OE?

TIME PARAMETERS

2-11. The amount of time allotted for the exercise must be one of the first decisions made before an OE can be designed or fitted to an exercise. The exercise planner must know the length of the exercise in order to develop situations and the fidelity of the OE. For example, if the exercise is only a few days, more information may have to be given to the training unit prior to the start in order for them to do their mission analysis and planning. If the exercise is longer, situations and events can have time to evolve and the training unit will have more opportunities to influence their environments. The exercise planner will be planning the buildup to key events and the consequences and effects of those key events. Depending on the time available, there may not be time to build up to a key event, and there may only be first- or second-order consequences after a key event.

TYPE OF EXERCISE

2-12. The Army's increased capability to integrate virtual and constructive simulations with live training, and the increased need for joint and multi-echelon training require exercise planners to develop a detailed and consistent OE for each training event. Defining the OE provides top-down coherence, flexibility, and continuity to the exercise and allows interaction at all levels. Depending on the particular training unit, the majority of training exercises will use a combination of live, virtual, constructive, and gaming (L-V-C-G) training enablers. For example, if a brigade combat team (BCT) trains at an MCTC, it may not have its full complement of troops available for the exercise and could be lacking its military intelligence company. Because a BCT cannot train effectively without its intelligence function, the military intelligence company could be simulated by having several intelligence experts communicate to the BCT through its normal communications and data transfer methods. Likewise, an aviation platoon may not have its normal equipment because of fielding or maintenance issues; so it could train virtually on a simulator, with the results transmitted to the BCT through normal communications and data transfer methods. This way, although all the troops and equipment are not available for the exercise, the unit is still able to complete effective collective training.

OPERATIONAL THEME

2-13. Selection of the operational theme(s) is a key decision that the exercise director needs to make during the initial planning phase. In coordination with the higher commander, this initial decision is normally completed during the preliminary planning sessions. The operational theme is the character of the dominant major operation being conducted at any time within a land force commander's area of operations. The operational theme helps convey the nature of the major operation to the force to facilitate common understanding of how the commander broadly intends to operate. (FM 3-0) Operational themes can be selected from the following:

- Major combat operations.
- Irregular warfare.
- Peace operations.
- Limited intervention.
- Peacetime military engagement.

2-14. The assignment of the operational theme for a training exercise is critical because it helps commanders identify the most important training tasks. It also helps provide the means to coordinate and integrate more focused supporting collective and individual tasks throughout the organization. Depending on the time allotted for the exercise, it may be possible to train sequentially under two different operational themes.

OPERATIONAL ENVIRONMENT ASSESSMENT

2-15. The decision on whether a training exercise will be based an existing OEA for an actual OE or a composite COE-based OE depends on whether the exercise is the based on a directed or contingency mission. For example, sometimes a training unit is assigned a contingency mission in a particular area of the world; so its training could be based on a real location and OE. Otherwise, the training unit would focus on honing its core tasks. Either way, the OEA is a tool to easily and effectively design the OE for the exercise. If a particular area of the world is the focus, the TRADOC G-2 Intelligence Support Activity (TRISA) has developed several OEAs that can be found on its website at https://www.us.army.mil/suite/files/14752839 (AKO access is required). The purpose of the OEAs on the TRISA website is twofold. Each OEA provides a detailed description and analysis of a specific OE and a model for the application of the operational variables (PMESII-PT) to support actual operations or exercises. The PMESII-PT variables, their subvariables, and related impacts are discussed, as well as potential trends in the OE. If no existing OEA corresponds to the OE desired for a particular training exercise, exercise planners can follow the methodology of these real-world examples to create an OEA for the OE associated with the desired geographical area. If an exercise does not require fidelity to an actual OE, exercise planners can modify an existing OEA or design their own composite OE. A composite OE is developed by selecting the subvariable or sub-subvariable settings (from a detailed list found in chapter 3) that best support the training objectives. If the training unit is only focusing on its core tasks, it can also use an existing OEA, modify an existing OEA, or it can design its own composite OE.

> *Note.* In order to meet specific training requirements or unit-requested conditions, the creation of any training event will normally include portions of existing, modified, or composite OEs regardless of whether training is for a contingency mission or core tasks.

PRODUCTS

2-16. Products resulting from the initial planning should be defined exercise design parameters based on available resources and METL-based prioritized training objectives.

SECTION II - PHASE 2: TASK AND COUNTERTASK DEVELOPMENT

2-17. The purpose of phase 2 is for exercise planners to examine the selected training tasks and conduct an OPFOR countertask analysis in order to counter or stress the training unit. During this phase, it is assumed that the commander of the U.S. unit to be trained has already identified the units he wants trained in the selected tasks.

WHO

2-18. The key players in this phase are the exercise planner and OPFOR commander. Depending on the size and type of exercise, the specific makeup of these planners may change. The OPFOR commander's role in an exercise may be two-fold. That is, he is required to command the OPFOR, but as a trainer he may act in a "white-hat" or neutral capacity for exercise control and the exercise director to ensure the training unit's training objectives are being met. He therefore may be privy to some aspects of the training unit's planning and operations, but required not to use the information to OPFOR tactical advantage. Regardless of who is involved, it is critical that both training unit and OPFOR planners coordinate closely during this phase in order to ensure a cohesive and productive training exercise.

TOOLS

2-19. The exercise planner must have the products from phase 1 (the defined exercise parameters and METL-based prioritized unit training objectives). He also must have TC 7-100 series publications and the OPFOR Tactical Task List (see appendix B).

> *Note.* If the nature of the exercise allows the exercise planner to develop the OPFOR OB, task organization, and equipment tier levels during phase 2, this could necessitate the use of the *Worldwide Equipment Guide* (WEG) as another tool. This tool is discussed under phase 2 only because this is the earliest phase in which it could possibly be used.

KEY DECISIONS

2-20. While training unit tasks are determined by the unit's METL, the supporting collective and individual tasks on which the exercise will focus must be carefully selected. This selection will drive the selection of appropriate OPFOR countertasks.

> *Note.* In some cases, the exercise planner may be able to proceed from OPFOR countertasks directly to the development of the OPFOR OB, task organization, and equipment tier levels during phase 2. Otherwise, those decisions may need to occur after OE development, in phase 3 or even in phase 4. These actions are discussed under phase 2 only because this is the earliest phase in which they could possibly occur. Even if these decisions are initially made in phase 2, they could be refined during a later phase.

OPFOR COUNTERTASKS

2-21. The OPFOR Tactical Task List (see appendix B) is a listing of OPFOR tactical countertasks. From this list, the exercise planner must select the countertasks that match the training unit's tasks. If, for example, the training unit's selected training objectives include overcoming barriers, obstacles and mines, the OPFOR countertask would involve creating barriers or obstacles or emplacing mines. If the training unit's tasks include air defense, then the OPFOR needs to have aviation unit tasks. If the training unit's tasks include counterinsurgency operations, then the OPFOR should include insurgent tasks. The exercise planner should develop OPFOR countertasks that—

- Oppose the training unit's training objectives in accordance with the OPFOR Tactical Task List.
- Reflect TC 7-100 series doctrine, organizations, and equipment (unless training for a specific contingency with a specific adversary).
- Are appropriate to the training unit troop list, expected training status, and area of operation (AO).

2-22. Once the OPFOR countertasks (or COAs) are selected, the exercise planner aligns training unit tasks with OPFOR countertasks to determine OPFOR missions. For example, in order to arrive at a training unit task of "Actions on Contact" and the OPFOR countertasks of ambush, improvised explosive device (IED), electronic warfare (EW), and indirect fire, the exercise planner studies the required supporting subtasks from the Army Universal Task List (AUTL) in FM 7-15, as shown in table 2-2, to determine what countertasks are required of the OPFOR.

Table 2-2. Example training unit supporting subtasks (actions on contact)

ART 1.2.2.7 CONDUCT ACTIONS ON CONTACT		
No.	**Scale**	**Measure**
01	Yes/No	Unit generated and sustained overwhelming combat power at the point of contact if the element that made contact was able to defeat the enemy unassisted.
02	Yes/No	The generation of overwhelming combat power was the product of the recommended course of action to the higher commander.
03	Yes/No	Intelligence, surveillance, and reconnaissance assets were used to develop situation wi hout main body being in contact with the enemy.
04	Time	To deploy and report.
05	Time	To evaluate and develop the situation.
06	Time	To choose a course of action (COA).
07	Time	To execute a selected COA.
08	Time	To recommend a COA to the higher commander.
09	Time	To return to previous mission.
10	Percent	Of friendly forces available to continue previous mission.
11	Percent	Of combat effectiveness of enemy force that made contact.

2-23. By studying the assigned task (actions on contact) and its supporting subtasks, the exercise planner can see that the OPFOR required must—

- Not start with overwhelming combat power, but can get there.
- Allow the training unit to use ISR assets to stay out of contact.
- Be able to challenge the training unit's ability to carry out its selected COA.
- Be able to cause the training unit to not be able to continue its mission.

2-24. In another example, the exercise planner studies the required training unit subtasks of "Conduct Joint Operations Area (JOA) Missile Defense," as shown in table 2-3, in order to determine what countertasks are required of the OPFOR. By studying the assigned task and its subtasks, the exercise planner can see that the OPFOR required must be able to employ ballistic, air-to-surface, and cruise missiles.

Table 2-3. Example of training unit task (JOA missile defense)

OP 6.1.5 CONDUCT JOINT OPERATIONS AREA (JOA) MISSILE DEFENSE

To identify and integrate joint and coalition forces supported by integrated capabilities to detect and destroy enemy theater missiles directed toward the JOA in flight or prior to launch. This task includes disrupting the enemy's theater missile operations through an appropriate mix of mutually supportive passive missile defense, active missile defense, attack operations, and supporting command, control, communications, computers, and intelligence (C4I) measures. This task includes providing early warning of theater missile attack to the joint operations area (JOA) as well as distribution of this warning to joint and multinational forces within the operational area. The term "theater missile" applies to ballistic missiles, air-to-surface missiles, and air-, land-, and sea-launched cruise missiles whose targets are within the joint force commander's (JFC's) operational area.

No.	Scale	Measure
M01	Minutes	Warning provided to friendly assets prior to threat arrival.
M02	Percent	Of attacking missiles successfully penetrated friendly defenses.
M03	Percent	Of launched air-to-surface missiles destroyed before impact.
M04	Percent	Of launched ballistic missiles destroyed before impact.
M05	Percent	Of launched cruise missiles destroyed before impact.
M06	Percent	Of theater assets defensible against theater missile threat.
M07	Percent	Of TMD capability damaged by incoming missile attacks.
M08	Percent	Of DAL locations defensible against theater missile threat.
M09	Percent	Of DAL locations, successfully defended.
M10	Instances	Of failure to apply passive missile defense procedures.

TMD = theater missile defense; DAL = defended asset list

OPFOR OB AND TASK ORGANIZATION

2-25. An important factor in the continuation of this phase is whether the training unit has a specific real-world OE and the type of exercise selected is deployment related, such as an MRX. If this is the case, then the exercise planner and/or OPFOR commander could continue with building an OPFOR OB to include task organization, since the OE or exercise conditions have already been established. The exception to this is if the deploying training unit also has the OB of the actual enemy force in sufficient resolution to use in conducting the MRX. However, if the training unit does not have a predefined OPFOR or OE, then the conditions for their exercise will have to be developed first, which will be discussed in the phase 3 (PMESII-PT OE development).

Note. Phase 2 is only the first of three phases in which OPFOR OB and task organization may be determined. The steps in the following example could be followed in phase 3 or even in phase 4.

2-26. Assuming that the training unit has defined OE conditions but does not have predetermined OB of the OPFOR for the exercise, the exercise planner would begin determining the appropriate type and size of OPFOR unit(s) capable of performing the OPFOR countertasks. The type of OPFOR unit is determined by the type of capability required for each OPFOR countertask. The size of the OPFOR organization is determined by the type of capability required and the size of the U.S. units(s) being trained. If, for example, the exercise is focused on major combat operations and the training unit will be attacking with two brigade-size units, then the OPFOR needs a brigade-size organization in order to provide an adequate defense. The optimal OPFOR organization for conducting such a defense, if the exercise is conducted in complex terrain, could include relatively light motorized infantry units with some mechanized infantry combined with an antiarmor capability. Such a mix of forces would include the use of a brigade tactical group (BTG) task organization. If an insurgency also exists in the OE, then a local insurgent force could also be included to provide the training unit with an opportunity to combat an insurgency. The insurgent force can either operate independently or become affiliated with the regular military force.

2-27. For the purpose of this example, only one guerrilla battalion will be resubordinated from its original parent insurgent organization to become an actual part of the BTG task organization. Because of its more military-like structure, this battalion can easily be incorporated into the BTG command structure and fight as a combat unit alongside the light motorized infantry. However, the remainder of the local insurgent organization remains only loosely affiliated with the BTG, rather than subordinate to it.

2-28. At this point, exercise planners review the OPFOR administrative force structure (AFS) organizational directories, which provide example equipment plus personnel types and the numbers of each type typically found in specific organizations. The AFS is to be used as the basis for OPFOR organization in all Army training exercises, except real-world-oriented MRXs. The AFS is the aggregate of various military headquarters, organizations, facilities, and installations designed to man, train, and equip the OPFOR. Within the AFS, tactical-level commands have standard organizational structures. The purpose of the AFS is to give trainers and exercise planners a general idea of what an OPFOR structure should look like. A complete list of AFS organizational directories, volumes I-IV, can be found at the U.S. Army Training and Doctrine Command (TRADOC) G2-TRISA Website at https://www.us.army.mil/suite/files/19296289 (AKO access required).

> **Note.** The AFS organizational directories are online files linked to FM 7-100.4. FM 7-100.4 provides detailed step-by-step instructions on how to construct a task organization in its chapter 3 and appendix B; its chapter 4 describes how to select equipment options.

2-29. From the AFS menu, exercise planners can compile an initial listing of OPFOR units for the task organization (see example in table 2-4). The purpose here is to review the OPFOR organizational directories to determine which standard OPFOR unit(s) most closely matches the type and size of units required for performing OPFOR countertasks. At this point, the initial list only identifies the units available, without concern for any higher-level command to which they are subordinate in the AFS. In most cases, the organizations found in the AFS will require task-organizing in order to construct an OPFOR OB appropriate for the exercise. Once selected, this OPFOR unit will become the base unit to which modifications are made.

Table 2-4. Example of initial listing of OPFOR units selected for task organization

• BTG Headquarters (based on Bde HQ)	• Sniper Company
• Motorized Infantry Battalion (x2)	• Air Defense Battalion (Motorized)
• Mechanized Infantry Battalion (APC)	• Engineer Battalion
• Guerrilla Battalion (Hunter-Killer)	• Materiel Support Battalion
• Antitank Battalion	• Maintenance Battalion (APC/Motorized)
• Artillery Battalion	• Signal Company
• Reconnaissance Battalion (Motorized)	• Chemical Defense Company
• SPF Company	• Medical Company
• SPF Deep Attack/Recon Platoon	

2-30. In the example in table 2-4, the exercise planner has determined that most of the units needed to conduct OPFOR countertasks can be found in the AFS organizational directory for a separate motorized infantry brigade. Therefore, that brigade will serve as the base unit for the required task organization, which will be a BTG based on that brigade's headquarters and some of its original subordinates in the AFS. However, OPFOR countertasks will also require the capabilities of some APC-equipped mechanized infantry, guerrilla forces, special-purpose forces (SPF), and additional snipers.

2-31. For the insurgent organization affiliated with the BTG in this example, the exercise planner would select the "Local Insurgent Organization" from the AFS organizational directories. He would then adjust the "default" numbers of the various function-oriented cells to tailor the organization to provide the desired insurgent tasks.

2-32. Before extracting the base unit from the organizational directories, exercise planners should determine how much of the organizational detail in the directories they actually need for their particular training exercise or simulation. The directories typically break out subordinate units down to squad-size components. However, some simulations either cannot or do not need to provide that level of resolution. Therefore, exercise planners should identify the lowest level of organization that will actually be portrayed. If the only task-organizing involved will be internal to that level of base unit, any internal task-organizing is transparent to the users. However, if any subordinate of that base unit receives assets from outside its immediate higher organization, it might be necessary to first modify the subordinate into a task organization and then roll up the resulting personnel and equipment totals into the totals for the parent organization in the OPFOR OB for the exercise.

2-33. Several decisions are involved in modifying the standard OPFOR baseline unit to become the new task organization. This can involve changes in subordinate units, equipment, and personnel. If training objectives do not require the use of all subordinates shown in a particular organization as it appears in the AFS, users can omit the subordinate units they do not need. Likewise, exercise planners can add other units to the baseline organization in order to create a task organization that is appropriate to training requirements. Users must ensure that the size and composition of the OPFOR is sufficient to meet training objectives and requirements. However, total assets organic to an organization or allocated to it from higher levels should not exceed that which is realistic and appropriate for the training scenario. Skewing the force ratio in either direction negates the value of training. Therefore, specific OBs derived from the organizational directories are subject to approval by the trainers' OPFOR-validating authority.

OPFOR TIER LEVELS

2-34. During the task-organizing process, adjustments in equipment may be necessary in order to modify the strength and capability of the OPFOR unit. If a particular piece of equipment shown in the AFS organizational directories is not appropriate for a specific scenario, exercise planners may substitute another system according to the guidelines in the *Worldwide Equipment Guide* (WEG). The WEG is organized into directories consisting of three volumes:

- Volume I, Ground Systems.
- Volume II, Airspace and Air Defense.
- Volume III, Naval and Littoral Systems.

The WEG is maintained and continuously updated, as necessary, by TRADOC G2-TRISA. Volumes I-III can be found at the TRADOC G2-TRISA Website at: https://www.us.army mil/suite/files/14751393 (AKO access required). It is important to note that even the baseline OPFOR organizations are subject to change over time. The equipment found in those organizations can also change. Therefore, planners should always consult the online AFS directories and the WEG for the latest, most up-to-date versions of organizational and equipment data.

2-35. The WEG contains equipment data, tier tables, and substitution matrices for the various categories of equipment found in OPFOR organizations. Exercise planners should exercise caution in modifying equipment holdings, since this impacts on an OPFOR unit's organizational integrity and combat capabilities.

2-36. Exercise planners can employ the tier tables and substitution matrices in the WEG to find appropriate substitutes for baseline equipment shown in the AFS organizational directories. Within each functional category of equipment, there are four tiers representing different levels of capability, with Tier 1 representing the highest level of capability and modernity. The four distinct tiers and their definitions are as follows:

- Tier 1 reflects systems across the different functional areas that a major military force with state-of-the-art technology would generally have. At Tier 1, new or upgraded systems are limited to those robust systems fielded in military forces or currently developed and marketed for sale, with capabilities and vulnerabilities that can be portrayed for training.

- Tier 2 reflects modern competitive systems fielded in significant numbers for the last 10 to 20 years, with limitations or vulnerabilities being diminished by available upgrades. Although forces are equipped for operations in all terrains and can fight day and night, their capability in range and speed for several key systems may be somewhat inferior to U.S. capability. Since the equipment listed in the AFS directories are Tier 2 equipment, any adjustments to equipment should be considered in light of this baseline structure.
- Tier 3 systems date back generally 30 to 40 years. They have limitations in all three subsystems categories: mobility, survivability, and lethality. Systems and force integration are inferior. However, guns, missiles, and munitions can still challenge vulnerabilities of U.S. forces. Selective upgrades can provide synergistic and adaptive increases in force effectiveness.
- Tier 4 systems reflect 40- to 50-year-old systems, some of which have been upgraded numerous times. These represent equipment typically found in forces of Third World or smaller developed countries. Use of effective strategy, adaptive tactics, selective technology upgrades, and terrain limitations could enable a Tier 4 OPFOR to challenge the effectiveness of a U.S. force in achieving its goals. This tier includes militia, guerrillas, special police, and other forces.

Note. No force in the world has all systems at the most modern tier. The OPFOR, as with all military forces worldwide, is a mix of legacy and modern systems. Thus, the typical OPFOR force comprises a mix of Tier 1-4 systems.

2-37. Table 2-5 provides a sample of systems listed in the tier tables (from volume I, chapter 15 of the WEG as of 2009). The characteristics of individual equipment listed can be found in the preceding chapters of volume I.

Table 2-5. Example of equipment listed in WEG tier tables

Equipment Type	Tier 1	Tier 2	Tier 3	Tier 4
Infantry Fighting Veh	BMP-2M Berezhok	BMP-2M	AMX-10P	BMP-1PG
Infantry FSV for IFV	BMP/Kliver AD/AT	BMP-2M Kornet/SA-18	AMX-10/SA-16/AT-5B	BMP-1PG w/ SA-16/AT-5
Armored Psnl Carrier	BTR-90	BTR-80A	BTR-80	M113A1
Amphibious APC/IFV	BTR/Kliver BMP/Kliver	BTR-80A/BMP-3 UAE	WZ-551/BMP-2	VTT-323/BMP-1PG
Infantry FSV for APC	BTR/Kliver AD/AT	BTR-80A/SA-18&Kornet	WZ-551/SA-16/AT-5B	BMP-1PG w/ SA-14/AT-5
Airborne APC/IFV	BTR-D/ BMD-3/Kliver	BTR-D/BMD-3	BTR-D/BMD-2	BTR-D/BMD-1P
Heavy IFV/Heavy IFSV	BMP-3M/BTR-90M/BMD-4	BMP-3 UAE	Marder 1A1	BMP-1PG
Main Battle Tank	T-90A	T-72B (Improved)	Chieftain	T-55AM
Amphibious Tank	Type 63A Modernized (AM)	Type 63AM	M1985	PT-76B
Tracked HACV	2S25	AMX-10 PAC 90	AMX-13EE-9	M41A3
Wheeled HACV	AMX-10RC Desert Storm	AMX-10RC	EE-9	EE-9
Combat Recon Veh	BRM-3K/Credo	BRM-3K	BRM-1K	EE-9
Abn/Amphib Recon CRV	BMD-3/Credo 1E	BMD-3K	BMD-1PK	BMD-1K
Armored Scout Car	BRDM-2M	BRDM-2M	Fox	BRDM-2
Sensor Recon Vehicle	HJ-62C	HJ-62C	BRM-1K	BRM-1K
AT Recon Vehicle	PRP-4M (TALL MIKE)	PRP-4M (TALL MIKE)	PRP-4 (TALL M KE)	PRP-3 (SMALL FRED)
Armored Cmd Veh	MP-21	BMP-1KSh	BMP-1KSh	BMP-1KS
Abn/Amphib ACV	BMD-1KShM	BMD-1KShM	BMD-1KShM	BMD-1KShM
Wheeled ACV	Kushetka-B	Kushetka-B	BTR-60PU/BTR-145BM	BTR-60PU/BTR-145BM
Command APC	BTR-90AK	BTR-80AK	BTR-60PBK	M113A1
Motorcycle	Gear-Up (2-man)	Gear-Up (2-man)	Motorcycle (2-man)	Motorcycle (2-man)
Tactical Utility Veh	VBR	VBL/VBR	UAZ-469	UAZ-469
Armrd Multi-purpose	MT-LB6MB	MT-LB6MA	MT-LBu	MT-LB
All-Terrain Vehicle	Supacat	Supacat	LUAZ-967M	LUAZ-967M

2-38. OPFOR organizations and equipment must support the entire spectrum of COE training scenarios for the U.S. Army. The OPFOR, as described in the TC 7-100 series, represents a variety of adversaries, and offers flexibility for use in training applications and scenarios for U.S. training. The main part of the WEG deals with systems that are widely proliferated in the current timeframe. Lists of equipment in the tier tables offer convenient baseline examples arranged in capability tiers for use in composing OPFOR equipment arrays for training scenarios. Each volume of the WEG also has a chapter on emerging technology trends. Tables in those chapters offer an extended capabilities tier for the near- and mid-term. Table 2-6 provides an example from an emerging technology trends chapter as of 2009.

Table 2-6. Example of emerging technology trends from WEG

System	Near-Term OPFOR (FY 09-13)	Mid-Term OPFOR (FY 14-19)
APC Air Defense/Antitank (ADAT) Vehicle	APC Bn and Bde MANPADS btry, selected other units	See A R DEFENSE
Infantry Fighting Vehicle	2-man turret, amphib tracked. Add ERA. 30mm gun (sabot, 110+mm pen). Frag-HE Electronic-fuzed ammo 5 km. Buckshot rd for UAVs. 40-mm ABM AGL, 4 x fiber-optic guided ATGM 8 km launch on move, 2nd gen FLIR. Auto-track, hunter-killer FCS. Remote MGs 12.7mm, 2 x 7 62. Laser designator 15 km. CPS/ATS	Hybrid drive. Box ERA 100mm KE /600 CE. 45-mm CTG. Fused FL R /II sight 13 km. ADAT dart rd 4 km. SAL/LBR ATGM 8-12 km. MMW radar. Micro-UAVs recon/atk. Radar warner, laser radar. Tunable LTD 15 km. CPS. 2 remote MGs, 1x 12.7. TV/ R attack grenades
FV ADAT Vehicle FV Bn/Bde MANPADS	FV chassis and APC ADAT weapons and upgrades	See A R DEFENSE, APC ADAT for weapons and upgrades
Heavy Infantry Fighting Vehicle (Heavy IFV in Heavy Bn, Infantry Fire Support Vehicle, or IFV Company Command Vehicle, as Required)	2-man turret, amphib tracked, Box ERA. Auto-track, hunter-killer FCS, ATGM lch on move. 100 and 30mm guns. 100mm HEAT, DPICM rounds. 40mm ABM AGL, NLOS (LBR/SAL) ATGM 8+km lch-on-move. 30/100mm HE electronic fuzed rd 7 km. 30-mm buckshot rd for UAVs. AD 12.7mm MG, 2 remote 7.62 MG. Laser designator 15 km. CPS/ATS	Hybrid drive. Armor and box ERA protects 300mm KE/800 CE. 45-mm CTG, KE, HE, ADAT rds. KE missile 8 km. Micro-UAVs recon/ atk. CPS. Fused FLIR/II sight 13 km. ATGM 8-12 km. Tunable laser designator to 15 km. Radar/ MMW warners. AGL, 2 remote MGs, 1x 12.7. TV/IR atk grds
HIFV ADAT Vehicle HIFV and Amphib Bn/Bde	HIFV chassis with APC ADAT weapons and upgrades	See A R DEFENSE, APC ADAT for weapons and upgrades
Main Battle Tank	Welded turret with more KE protection. 125mm gun, bigger sabot (800+mm), LBR ATGM 6 km. SAL-H/ R-homing HEAT rd 5 km in 1 sec, SAL-H ATGM 8 km. LTD to 10 km. Controls tank robot. 2nd gen FLIR (7 km) and 50X Day/night sights. ATGM fire on move. Auto-tracker, laser radar, laser dazzler blind sights. Focused frag HE rd for heli, AT targets. HEAT-MP, DPICM submunition rds. R/MMW CM. CPS/ATS	Reduced turret, compartmented rds, electromagnetic/ceramic armor, 3 gen ERA, 500 mm top/mine armor. Laser/radar warners. CPS. Hybrid drive. Sabot defeats 1000mm KE. Tunable laser LTD to 15 km. ADAT msl 8 km. Medium laser weapon. Fused FL R/II sight 100 X to 13 km. MMW FC. Atk/recon micro-UAV, atk grds. Controls a robot tank.

PRODUCTS

2-39. The products always resulting from phase 2 are the OPFOR countertasks developed from selected training unit tasks. In some cases, phase 2 may also include the consequent development of OPFOR OB, task organization, and equipment tier levels. As mentioned previously, those would only be developed during this phase if the OE was already defined but the OPFOR units were not defined. In that case, the entire process of phase 2 could result in building the appropriate OPFOR OB, which must provide suitable organizations capable of countering those tasks selected from the AUTL or UJTL for the training unit. For training units that do have an existing OE and defined OPFOR, the exercise planner would only develop countertasks during this phase. For training units that do not have a defined OE, the exercise planner must first develop an appropriate OE in phase 3 before he can define the OPFOR.

SECTION III - PHASE 3: PMESII-PT OPERATIONAL ENVIRONMENT DEVELOPMENT

2-40. An *operational environment* (OE) is a composite of the conditions, circumstances, and influences that affect the employment of capabilities and bear on the decisions of the commander (JP 3-0). Because this term was first introduced and defined in a Joint Pub about joint operations, a common misconception is that the term *operational environment* equates only to the operational level of war and that the "operational variables" used to describe an OE are applicable only at the operational or joint level. Both of those views are incorrect. The "operational" in both terms simply means that they relate to an operation, at any level. Every commander, at every level, has his own specific OE, which is part of the OE of his parent command

and includes the OEs of his subordinate commands. A specific mission occurs within the context of a specific OE.

2-41. At this point, the exercise planner has analyzed and integrated the exercise parameters and OPFOR countertasks. The next step is to match the results of phases 1 and 2 to the appropriate OE conditions for the training scenario. **This step is critical because it essentially creates the conditions for the selected unit training objectives.** These conditions, when combined with the standards for the METL task, help commanders assess unit readiness for a mission. Upon completion of this phase, all the conditions for the training exercise are set.

TOOLS

2-42. In the exercise is based on an existing OEA (for an actual operation or for an existing training scenario), that OEA is the foundation for phase 3. Depending on training requirements, the exercise planner may draw the necessary conditions directly from the existing OEA, develop more specific conditions for the specific OE of a smaller unit within that broader OE, or otherwise modify the existing OEA. If the exercise is not based on an existing OEA, the first step would be to create a composite OE that is appropriate for the training objectives, training unit tasks, and OPFOR countertasks already selected. In any case, the primary tool for this phase is to apply the framework of the eight operational variables and select appropriate settings for the subvariables.

OPERATIONAL VARIABLES (PMESII-PT)

2-43. The Army's increased capability to integrate virtual, gaming, and constructive simulations with live training, along with the increased need for joint and multi-echelon training, requires exercise planners to develop a detailed and consistent OE for each training event. Defining the OE provides top-down coherence, flexibility, and continuity to the exercise and allows interaction at all levels. **Most importantly, the operational variables of PMESII-PT (political, military, economic, social, information, infrastructure, physical environment, and time) and their interaction provide the analytical framework for establishing conditions at all levels of training.** The complexity of a specific OE in training can also be adjusted to ensure training objectives are met.

2-44. The framework for analysis of any OE should always consist of all eight operational variables that determine the nature of an OE and how it will affect an operation. The following is a brief description of each PMESII-PT variable, along with an example of questions a small-unit commander might need to have answered about each variable in his particular OE (in parentheses):

- **Political.** Describes the distribution of responsibility and power at all levels of governance—formally constituted authorities, as well as informal or covert political powers. (Who is the tribal leader in the village?)
- **Military.** Explores the military and/or paramilitary capabilities of all relevant actors (enemy, friendly, and neutral) in a given OE. (Does the enemy in this particular neighborhood have anti-tank missiles?)
- **Economic.** Encompasses individual and group behaviors related to producing, distributing, and consuming resources. (Does the village have a high unemployment rate that makes it easy for the enemy to get villagers to perform tasks for pay or other benefits?)
- **Social.** Describes the cultural, religious, and ethnic makeup within an OE and the beliefs, values, customs, and behaviors of society members. (Who are the influential people in the village—for example, religious leaders, tribal leaders, warlords, criminal bosses, or prominent families?)
- **Information.** Describes the nature, scope, characteristics, and effects of individuals, organizations, and systems that collect, process, disseminate, or act on information. (How much access does the local population have to news media or the internet?)
- **Infrastructure.** Is composed of the basic facilities, services, and installations needed for the functioning of a community or society. (Is the electrical generator in the village working?)

- **Physical Environment.** Includes the geography and man-made structures as well as the climate and weather in the area of operations. (What types of terrain or weather conditions in this AO favor enemy operations?)
- **Time.** Describes the timing and duration of activities, events, or conditions within an OE, as well as how the timing and duration are perceived by various actors in the OE. (At what times are people likely to congest roads or conduct activities that provide a cover for hostile operations?)

PMESII-PT SUBVARIABLES

2-45. Each of the eight PMESII-PT variables also has associated subvariables. A complete list of subvariables in detail is in chapter 3. Each subvariable listed there contains a subvariable definition and a breakdown of several distinct settings in order to develop specific exercise conditions. Each subvariable setting also has a corresponding definition, as well as associated planning considerations and notes to include links to other associated variables and subvariables. However, these are not always linked to a specific setting. (For an example of a subvariable, see table 2-7.)

Table 2-7. "Political: Type of Government" subvariable definition, settings, and setting definitions

Definition: Determines the type of government structure and associated behaviors encountered.		
Subvariable Setting	**Setting Definition**	**Considerations and Additional Notes**
Dictatorship/Authoritarian	A mode of government characterized by the existence of a single ruler or group who arrogate to themselves and monopolize power in the state, exercising it without restraint.	For live training requires robust domestic security apparatus, bureaucratic institutions and bloated role-player government structure (1.5 normal manning).
Theocracy	A government ruled by or subject to religious authority. A system of government in which God or a deity is held to be the civil ruler.	Can only occur in the first two categories of social religious diversity.
Representative Government	Characterized as a representative form of government—either democratic, republic or parliamentary in form—with elected representatives and executives. All politics are governed by will of people and government has limited, defined powers over the population.	Can be democratic, republic or parliamentary. Requires specific, prominent influencers, council members be present in the scenario (in addition to the normal role-player government positions).
Anarchy	Absence of any form of political authority. Political disorder and confusion. Absence of any cohesive principle, such as a common standard or purpose.	Tribal and religious role-players present in scenario. Small percentage of disenfranchised or former government officials with little influence.
Subvariable Links: Economic: Illegal Economic Activity; Social: Education Level, Religious Diversity, Criminal Activity.		

2-46. Ultimately the exercise planner is responsible for choosing the combination of subvariables for the exercise. Table 2-8 on page 2-14 provides an overview of the PMESII-PT variables and all their associated subvariables.

Table 2-8. PMESII-PT variables and subvariables

Political Variable	Information Variable	Time Variable
• Attitude toward the United States • Centers of political power • Type of government • Government effectiveness and legitimacy • Influential political groups	• Public communications media • Information warfare • Intelligence • Information management	• Knowledge of the AO • Cultural perception of time • Key event resolution • Information offset • Tactical exploitation of time • Key dates, time periods, or events
Military Variable • Military forces • Government paramilitary forces • Non-state paramilitary forces • Unarmed combatants • Nonmilitary armed combatants • Military functions	**Infrastructure Variable** • Construction pattern • Urban zones • Urbanized building density • Utilities present • Utility level • Transportation architecture	

Economic Variable
• Economic diversity
• Employment status
• Economic activity
• Illegal economic activity
• Banking and finance
	Physical Environment Variable
	• Terrain
	  ▪ Observation and fields of fire
	  ▪ Avenues of approach
	  ▪ Key terrain
	  ▪ Obstacles
	  ▪ Cover and concealment
	  ▪ Landforms
	  ▪ Vegetation
	  ▪ Terrain complexity
	  ▪ Mobility classification	

Social Variable
• Demographic mix
• Social volatility
• Education level
• Ethnic diversity
• Religious diversity
• Population movement
• Common languages
• Criminal activity
• Human rights
	• Natural hazards
	• Climate
	• Weather
	  ▪ Precipitation
	  ▪ High temperature—heat index
	  ▪ Low temperature—wind chill index
	  ▪ Wind
	  ▪ Visibility
	  ▪ Cloud cover
	  ▪ Relative humidity	

2-47. The eight variables and their associated subvariables describe the OE in terms that relate to specific situations as well as threat capabilities. **These variables are relevant to every echelon of command and are relevant to every military operation.** While individual variables do not dominate every environment, they are all present and require careful consideration. **The PMESII-PT variables produce a coherent profile of the exercise conditions that can be applied to multi-level training exercises and small-unit (brigade and below) training exercises alike.**

OPERATIONAL ENVIRONMENT ASSESSMENT

2-48. The purpose of an OEA is to understand all relevant aspects (conditions, circumstances, and influences) of a particular, specific OE for an actual operation or a training event. An OEA is a systematic examination of all eight operational variables (PMESII-PT) and the subvariables that make up each of those variables. An OEA also identifies interrelationships among the variables and subvariables, as well as potential trends over time.

2-49. The exercise planner can either use an existing OEA (for an actual OE or a composite OE used in previous exercises), modify an existing OEA, or create an OEA for a new OE tailored to the requirements of the planned exercise. By using an existing OEA, the PMESII-PT variables and subvariable settings are pre-set. By adjusting an existing OEA, the exercise planners can change specific subvariable settings to meet requested training objectives or specified conditions in the OE. However, a composite OE can also be built by the exercise planner by selecting the desired subvariable settings straight from chapter 3.

2-50. The subvariable settings have definable differences that result in unique characteristics or planning factors. Their characteristics also directly impact on the ability of a unit to accomplish its mission in an operation or in training. The exercise director is ultimately responsible for approving the combination of settings for the exercise.

2-51. The operational variables can describe conditions of a composite OE created for an exercise but are equally applicable to describing real-world OEs as required for mission rehearsal training. The OEA, depending on the required resolution of the exercise, can be an invaluable tool in determining the proper subvariable settings to produce the desired OE. Now that the exercise planner has developed the parameters of the exercise as well as established training unit tasks and OPFOR countertasks, he has the tools and products necessary to develop the exercise's OE, the foundation of the scenario.

ORDER OF CONSIDERATION

2-52. PMESII-PT is the memory aid for the eight operational variables that make up any OE. When listing the variables, it is therefore advisable to list them in the same order as in the memory aid—to ensure that all are considered. The same is generally true for their order as headings, for instance in an OEA. However, that does not mean that one always addresses and analyzes the variables in that particular order. The order in which variables are considered may depend on several things, including—

- Whether a training exercise will use live, virtual, constructive, and or gaming enablers.
- Whether the operational theme(s) selected for the exercise require specific conditions in one or more variables.
- Whether one is analyzing an actual OE, modifying an actual OE, or creating a composite OE for training.
- Whether the training unit has requested specific conditions in which to perform tasks.

Training Enablers

2-53. One of the key decisions that must be made during phase 1 is the type of exercise—whether the exercise will be live, virtual, constructive, gaming, or a combination of those training enablers. This decision may affect the order in which variables are considered. For example, if the exercise (or part of it) is to be conducted in a live training venue, much of the Physical Environment variable is predetermined. The terrain, natural hazards, climate, and weather are whatever actually exists at the live training venue. When virtual, constructive, or gaming enablers are involved, the Physical Environment might be considered only after settings for other variables have been determined.

Operational Themes

2-54. The choice of operational theme or a combination of themes and the tasks inherent in them may cause emphasis on certain operational variables. Commanders must understand the OE for an operation in terms of the operational variables and describe their desired end state in terms of how they envision the conditions of the OE when the operation ends. This affects their focus on certain tasks and certain operational variables or subvariables related to those tasks. For example, foreign humanitarian assistance operations within an operational theme of limited intervention might cause exercise planners to place special emphasis on the Social and Economic variables and possibly the "natural hazards" subvariable of the Physical Environment variable. Thus, exercise planners might choose to consider such key variables first.

Actual, Modified, or Composite OE

2-55. Another key decision in phase 1 is whether the scenario will be based on an existing OEA for an actual OE or a composite OE. The type of OE being analyzed will determine the relative importance of individual operational variables and the order in which they should be considered. The order may be different for conducting an OEA for an actual OE than for using the operational variables as a tool to design a modified or composite OE for training.

Actual OE

2-56. By using an existing OEA, the PMESII-PT variables and subvariable settings are pre-set. For an actual OE, the characteristics of all the variables are determined by the actual situation in the particular part of the world in which an operation is taking place or could take place. In this case, the purpose of an OEA is to help understand all the relevant aspects of that particular OE—most likely starting with the basic Physical Environment of the selected geographic area. Even when doing an OEA for a contingency operation, the general physical location—the *where* of the operation—is known. Until an actual mission is received, the *when* of the operation (part of the Time variable) may not be known. Even without knowing the specific time, however, the commander and staff can begin the OEA process—assessing the nature and impact of all the other variables as they exist at the present and as they continue to evolve over time. The variables and their subvariables might be considered in order of available information.

2-57. In a particular actual OE, one or more operational variables might obviously have a greater impact on operations than others. In that case, one might want to consider those variables first, in order to be able to assess how they will influence other variables.

Note. PMESII-PT should always be used in analyzing an OE regardless of whether or not the training unit has a specified OE. Even an existing OEA does not always have the appropriate level of resolution for the type or level of training exercise that may desired. PMESII-PT provides the comprehensive framework necessary for the development of the conditions for any level and type of training.

Modified OE

2-58. The order of consideration may be different when modifying an existing OE (for an actual operation or a previous training exercise) to meet specific training requirements and/or resource constraints. Most characteristics of the variables are a given, determined by the nature of those aspects of an OE that has already been analyzed. By adjusting an existing OEA, the exercise planner can change specific subvariable settings to meet specified training objectives or requested conditions in the OE. The order of consideration may depend on the exercise parameters, which will determine how closely the OE for training can or should replicate the actual conditions of the actual OE. Training objectives may necessitate adding, deleting, or modifying some conditions (when considering tasks, conditions, and standards). Resources constraints will determine where risk must be accepted and where intelligent compromise will be necessary.

Composite OE

2-59. If one is creating a composite OE, the exercise parameters will drive the order in which variables are considered. Since training objectives are driven by METL, certain supporting tasks for the training unit will drive the countertasks selected for the OPFOR. The OPFOR countertasks could determine the basic characteristics of the Military variable up front. As exercise planning continues, planners would refine their design of the OPFOR, creating the appropriate OPFOR OB and task organization—all part of the Military variable. In this case, the consideration of the rest of the variables could follow the decisions about the Military variable and would provide conditions that appropriately interact with those of the Military variable to produce the desired training results. However, some training unit tasks might not correspond to an OPFOR countertask, but rather to some other condition in the OE used for training (for example, a failed government or natural disaster). In such cases, those variables might be considered first or early in the process of developing the OE.

KEY DECISIONS

2-60. During phase 3, the exercise planner must select the appropriate subvariable settings for each of the operational variables. He must ensure that the selected settings reinforce the specific OE conditions the training unit requires. He must also determine the common processes and key events that help portray the OE conditions and their impact on the training unit.

SUBVARIABLE SELECTION EXAMPLE

2-61. The following is an extended example that follows the logic of how one exercise planner might select the subvariable settings to meet requirements for a particular exercise. Obviously, these are not the only settings possible. Likewise, the order in which the planner in this example considers the eight operational variables is only one example of one possible order in which an exercise planner might address the variables.

2-62. For the purpose of this example, the exercise planner is selecting subvariable settings for an exercise that is not an MRX with a specified AO and will not use a live training environment. However the exercise parameters may indicate a requirement to create a particular type of geographical area to conduct the exercise. For example, the exercise planner could need to develop an OE centered around an AO in which the Physical Environment variable—

- Provides terrain that accomplishes terrain-based training objectives (for example, river crossing and urban operations).
- Provides terrain appropriate to the troop list.
- Provides conditions that stress command, control, and logistics.

2-63. Once these exercise parameters have been taken into account, the exercise planner in this example could begin by selecting the subvariable settings for the Physical Environment variable. At this point, the planner is trying to establish realistic conditions, using the PMESII-PT variables, which will stress all anticipated operations and requirements. For example (see figure 2-1), the exercise planner may choose the "mixed" setting for the "landforms" subvariable of the Physical Environment variable. Since the setting definition of "mixed" is "two or more ... landforms comprising over 80% of the available terrain in an AO," the planner may select "mountain/glacial" in the eastern portion of the country and "coastal" in the western side of the country. It follows then that the associated "climate" subvariable settings selected for this AO would be "oceanic" in the west and "subarctic" in the east. Since the planner may also want to ensure that the physical environment accommodates the maneuver of mechanized and armor formations and is open enough to allow long-range engagements, he may also select a "grassland" setting of the "vegetation" subvariable of the Physical Environment variable. This in turn would require the planner to also define "cover and concealment" as generally poor except in mountainous regions.

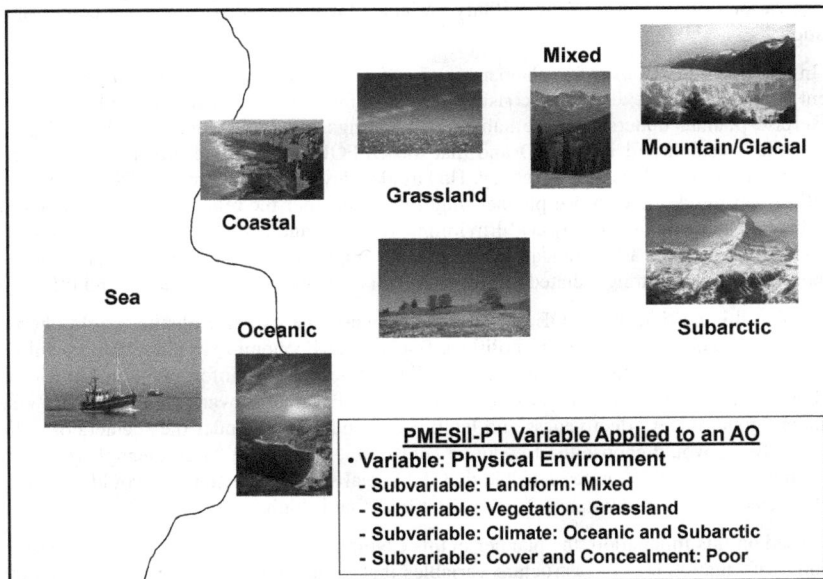

Figure 2-1. Selecting an area of operations (example)

2-64. Next the exercise planner in this example could continue developing the OE using the variable of Time. One of the more important subvariables of Time is "knowledge of the AO." This subvariable defines the amount of information the training unit will have received before the exercise begins, based on the amount of time they have spent in the AO (according to the scenario). If, for example, the training unit does not have detailed knowledge of the AO and OE, the planner could select "established," which means the unit in the scenario is midway through its tour of duty and has only moderate knowledge of the AO and OE. Additional time subvariables that should also be considered are "key-event resolution" and "information offset." Key-event resolution defines the number of key events and orders of effect to be designed into the scenario in order to accomplish unit training objectives. Information offset is the percentage of significant OPFOR activities that will be presaged by sufficient tips or indicators in order to enable successful training on unit reaction or interdiction response to the designed events.

2-65. If, as in this example, the Physical Environment and Time variables are determined first, those variables will shape and define the rest of the variables. The exercise planner then begins to complete the design of the OE by reviewing chapter 3 to determine the appropriate subvariable settings for the remaining variables. Again, the exercise planner tries to find the best fit to support the scenario and the training objectives.

2-66. At this point in the process, the exercise planner could develop the capabilities of the OPFOR by selecting the applicable subvariables of the Military variable. Using the countertasks already established in phase 2, the planner begins by selecting the type of military forces he will use in the exercise in order to field a challenging and capable OPFOR. Since we already know that the physical environment in the ongoing example was designed for major combat operations, it follows that the OPFOR selected, within the subvariable of "military forces," would be "predominately tank and mechanized infantry." Once this is determined, the next step would be to determine the degree to which this OPFOR can perform various "military functions," which is also a subvariable of Military. The planner would then select the appropriate setting for each function, such as fire support or maneuver, using a scale of "high," "medium," or "low." In the example discussed in the previous paragraphs, the planner may select "medium," which means the OPFOR can conduct limited, complex, synchronized tasks, is limited primarily to the theater of operations in its ability to influence friendly forces, and has predominantly Tier 2 equipment. (See chapter 3 on the Military variable for details.) If the exercise design also requires an insurgency, the planner would continue selecting various subvariables of the Military variable that specifically address the composition of this organization.

2-67. In our example, the exercise planner has already established subvariable settings for a physical environment suitable for the exercise by considering the training objectives and troop list of the training unit. The exercise planner understands the subvariable settings and implications of Time. He knows that the training unit is established in the AO and that the OPFOR will include the capability to conduct major combat operations as well as an insurgency. He has also developed his tentative COAs for the training unit. With all this in mind, the exercise planner might next consider the relationship and connectivity between the established subvariables of Physical Environment, Time, and Military and the remaining variables. Using these three variables as a foundation, the planner might then analyze their impact when selecting the remaining subvariable settings related to Political, Social, Economic, Information, and Infrastructure.

2-68. During this portion of the OE development process, the exercise planner might choose to first address the subvariable settings for the Political, Social, and Economic variables. This would allow him to build a foundation from which he can then develop the appropriate Information and Infrastructure conditions. For example, the planner might wish to choose the Political subvariable settings of "vulnerable: failing" under "government effectiveness and legitimacy" and "tribal" under the "centers of political power." Consequently, he would choose the Economic subvariable settings of "high unemployment" and a "single industry present." It is then quite plausible that the Social subvariable settings would be a relatively young or "unbalanced, age" population and "social volatility" that is high.

2-69. Based on this foundation, the planner in this example would then select subvariable settings from the remaining Information and Infrastructure variables that logically match the other OE conditions selected. For example, the Information variable would probably have a "public communications media" subvariable that has widespread "postal" and "radio" with limited "Internet" and "television." The "information management" subvariable setting would probably be either "rudimentary" or "basic." Finally, appropriate subvariable settings for the Infrastructure variable would be selected. Since the training unit in this example wants an insurgency as part of the design, the planner would ensure that selected Infrastructure settings included "dense, random construction" and "high" building density, as well as urban zones that include a "city core" and a "high-rise residential area." This would allow for an insurgency to operate using cities as cover as well as provide a training platform for urban operations.

2-70. Once the overall OE has been developed using the PMESII-PT variables, the exercise planner or OPFOR planner could begin building the appropriate OPFOR OB details and task organization covered previously in phase 2. For the ongoing example, this would include the conventional OPFOR units as well as the insurgent organizations, using the appropriate TC 7-100 series and associated documents described earlier.

OE-WFF ANALYSIS

2-71. The success or failure of any mission may be determined by the comprehensiveness of the METL's supporting tasks. If the commander is not aware of shortfalls in the task organization, planning, or training, he cannot address or alleviate them. Therefore, it is imperative that the commander have all-inclusive, across-the-board supporting METL tasks to guide planning and training and to highlight any issues requiring resolution. A comprehensive METL and associated tasks must consider all aspects of any issue(s) that may affect the accomplishment of the mission. This includes, but is not limited to, organizational shortfalls and capabilities and the defined OE using the PMESII-PT framework described above. Once these are analyzed and highlighted, the commander is then able to assign priorities and resources to each area.

2-72. Although other factors also affect the selection of the METL tasks, at a minimum well developed METL tasks must integrate the mission, the defined OE, and the warfighting functions (WFFs). This integration can be accomplished by taking into consideration the conditions, circumstances, and influences of the PMESII-PT variables in relation to the WFFs and the assigned mission. What is required is an analytical tool that fuses all these critical issues of interest to the commander. A convenient tool for this analysis is an OE-WFF analysis matrix. Filling in such a matrix should help identify conditions that may require adjustments to the original unit METL tasks and organization developed in phase 1. The requirements revealed in such an analytical matrix result in a comprehensive list of supporting tasks (including tasks of the basic table of organization and equipment [TOE] organization and newly added task-organized subordinates). The results provide an inclusive adjusted baseline that reveals critical METL supporting tasks for the commander's review and approval.

2-73. To illustrate this process, figure 2-2 provides a new example of notional BCT METL supporting tasks. These were specific Army tactical tasks (ARTs) that were selected from the AUTL found in FM 7-15 prior to applying the OE-WFF analysis matrix.

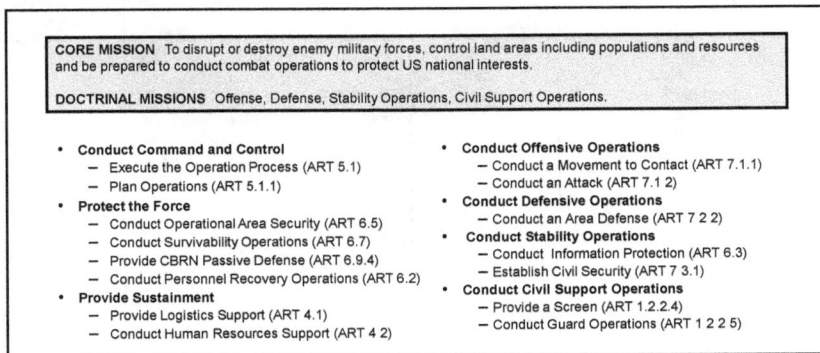

CORE MISSION To disrupt or destroy enemy military forces, control land areas including populations and resources and be prepared to conduct combat operations to protect US national interests.

DOCTRINAL MISSIONS Offense, Defense, Stability Operations, Civil Support Operations.

- **Conduct Command and Control**
  - Execute the Operation Process (ART 5.1)
  - Plan Operations (ART 5.1.1)
- **Protect the Force**
  - Conduct Operational Area Security (ART 6.5)
  - Conduct Survivability Operations (ART 6.7)
  - Provide CBRN Passive Defense (ART 6.9.4)
  - Conduct Personnel Recovery Operations (ART 6.2)
- **Provide Sustainment**
  - Provide Logistics Support (ART 4.1)
  - Conduct Human Resources Support (ART 4 2)

- **Conduct Offensive Operations**
  - Conduct a Movement to Contact (ART 7.1.1)
  - Conduct an Attack (ART 7.1 2)
- **Conduct Defensive Operations**
  - Conduct an Area Defense (ART 7 2 2)
- **Conduct Stability Operations**
  - Conduct Information Protection (ART 6.3)
  - Establish Civil Security (ART 7 3.1)
- **Conduct Civil Support Operations**
  - Provide a Screen (ART 1.2.2.4)
  - Conduct Guard Operations (ART 1 2 2 5)

Figure 2-2. Notional BCT METL with doctrinal supporting tasks (example)

2-74. Using this notional METL and doctrinal supporting tasks as a baseline, the exercise planner then builds an OE-WFF analysis matrix using the assumed data already compiled from the PMESII-PT variables analyzed against doctrinal WFFs. (See table 2-9 on page 2-20.) Using this construct, the initial supporting tasks are evaluated to determine if they do or do not correspond to the new conditions (PMESII-PT). In addition, the OE-WFF analysis matrix is used to determine if other supporting tasks need to be added.

Table 2-9. OE-WFF analysis matrix (example)

		WARFIGHTING FUNCTIONS					
		Movement and Maneuver	Intelligence	Fires	Sustainment	C2	Protection
OPERATIONAL VARIABLES	*Political*						• *Government unstable* • *Active insurgency*
	Military	• *Robust antiarmor (a)* • **Deploy within 96 hours (b)** • **Provide air support (c)** • *IEDs* • **Insufficient river-crossing capability**	• **Limited HUMINT capability** • **No UAVs assigned**	• *Limited line of sight*	• **Insufficient POL & water trucks to support task force**	• **Poor UHF/VHF radio relay**	• *Robust air defense (c)* • *Suicide bombers* • **No CBRN capability** • **Insufficient medical personnel and supplies**
	Economic		• *High unemployment*		• *Strong black market economy*		• *Strong illegal drug trade*
	Social		• *Tribal based*	• *Numerous no-fire zones* • *Significant number of religious structures*	• **Water for 5,000 troops & vehicles (d)** • *No water or food avail for 15,000 locals (d)*		
	Information		• **Establish HUMINT operations w/in 10 days** • *Active intelligence service*			• *Robust INFOWAR, EW, cyber capability* • *Large NGO presence*	
	Infrastructure	• *Limited hard surface roads* • **Insufficient cross-country vehicles** • **Heavy reliance on air transport** • **Insufficient mine-clearing & river-crossing capabilities**			• *Lack of potable water, POL, lodging, plumbing*	• *Limited electric power* • *No cell towers*	
	Physical Environment	• *Numerous rivers* • *Swamp/marsh* • *Cold* • *Mountainous* • *Unexploded explosive ordnance*		• *Limited fields of fire*	• *Limited natural water/2-year drought (d)*	• *Limited line of sight*	• *Diseases (typhoid & malaria)*
	Time	• **Extended road movement**	• **Limited AO knowledge**				
		BLUE: Capabilities and limitations in light of directed mission and OE conditions					
		RED (italics): OPFOR and other characteristics of operational variables					

NOTES:
(a) Robust insurgent antiarmor/antitank ability. Possess Kornet-E, RPG-29, RPG-7V1.
(b) Deploy to *Country X* **within 96 hours.**
(c) Robust insurgent air defense weapons. Starstreak, SA-16/SA-18.
(d) **Water/food for 5,000 troops & vehicles.** *Local population of 15,000 has limited food and contaminated water supply and is malnourished.*

2-75. Analyzing this information can result in several changes to the initial supporting METL tasks. (Figure 2-3 shows an example of notional BCT METL supporting tasks adjusted for OE and WFF.)

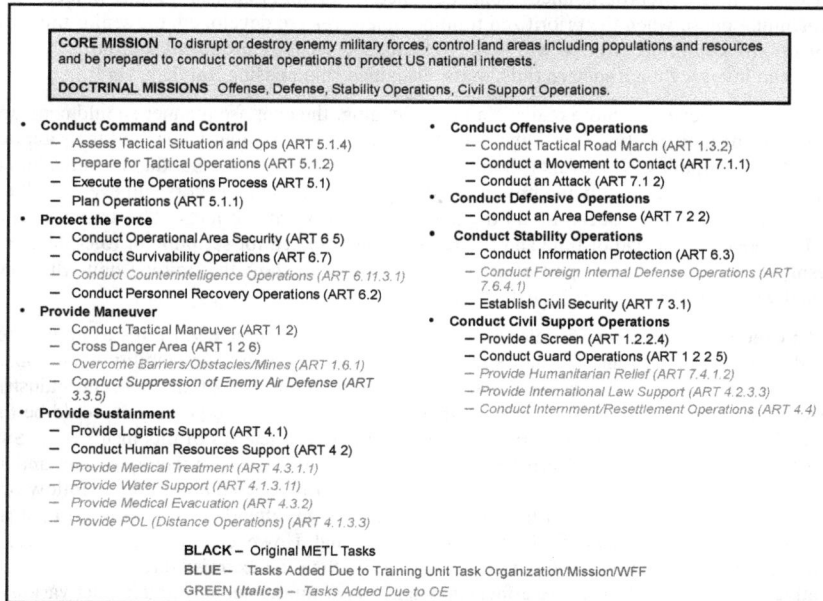

CORE MISSION To disrupt or destroy enemy military forces, control land areas including populations and resources and be prepared to conduct combat operations to protect US national interests.

DOCTRINAL MISSIONS Offense, Defense, Stability Operations, Civil Support Operations.

- **Conduct Command and Control**
  - Assess Tactical Situation and Ops (ART 5.1.4)
  - Prepare for Tactical Operations (ART 5.1.2)
  - Execute the Operations Process (ART 5.1)
  - Plan Operations (ART 5.1.1)
- **Protect the Force**
  - Conduct Operational Area Security (ART 6 5)
  - Conduct Survivability Operations (ART 6.7)
  - *Conduct Counterintelligence Operations (ART 6.11.3.1)*
  - Conduct Personnel Recovery Operations (ART 6.2)
- **Provide Maneuver**
  - Conduct Tactical Maneuver (ART 1 2)
  - Cross Danger Area (ART 1 2 6)
  - *Overcome Barriers/Obstacles/Mines (ART 1.6.1)*
  - *Conduct Suppression of Enemy Air Defense (ART 3.3.5)*
- **Provide Sustainment**
  - Provide Logistics Support (ART 4.1)
  - Conduct Human Resources Support (ART 4 2)
  - *Provide Medical Treatment (ART 4.3.1.1)*
  - *Provide Water Support (ART 4.1.3.11)*
  - *Provide Medical Evacuation (ART 4.3.2)*
  - *Provide POL (Distance Operations) (ART 4.1.3.3)*

- **Conduct Offensive Operations**
  - Conduct Tactical Road March (ART 1.3.2)
  - Conduct a Movement to Contact (ART 7.1.1)
  - Conduct an Attack (ART 7.1 2)
- **Conduct Defensive Operations**
  - Conduct an Area Defense (ART 7 2 2)
- **Conduct Stability Operations**
  - Conduct Information Protection (ART 6.3)
  - *Conduct Foreign Internal Defense Operations (ART 7.6.4.1)*
  - Establish Civil Security (ART 7 3.1)
- **Conduct Civil Support Operations**
  - Provide a Screen (ART 1.2.2.4)
  - Conduct Guard Operations (ART 1 2 2 5)
  - *Provide Humanitarian Relief (ART 7.4.1.2)*
  - *Provide International Law Support (ART 4.2.3.3)*
  - *Conduct Internment/Resettlement Operations (ART 4.4)*

BLACK – Original METL Tasks

BLUE – Tasks Added Due to Training Unit Task Organization/Mission/WFF

GREEN (Italics) – Tasks Added Due to OE

Figure 2-3. Notional BCT METL supporting tasks adjusted for OE and WFF (example)

2-76. First, a task such as "Provide CBRN Passive Defense" can be deleted because, in this case, the OPFOR does not have a CBRN capability. Second, tasks such as "Provide Water Support" and "Provide Humanitarian Relief" have been added due to the humanitarian crisis in the OE. Issues, relationships, and cascading effects, not obvious with a stand-alone METL, become evident once combined with specifics unique to the assigned mission, the task organization, and the defined OE. Once all aspects are considered in one analytical process, the differences in the BCT supporting task list are significant, and obvious. This methodology provides the commander a tailored, all-encompassing tool to assess both the unit's readiness and its ability to perform the directed mission in the form of adjusted supporting METL tasks based on OE-WFF analysis.

2-77. Once the OE has been determined, then further decisions and development can be made on the scenario. These include common processes and key events for the desired scenario.

COMMON PROCESSES

2-78. An integral part of the scenario is the everyday activity that brings the scenario to life, making it a realistic training environment that forces the training unit to react and think through the ramifications of its actions. In order to understand this OE that appears so complicated, the exercise planner utilizes a method of preplanned events that are common to all exercise OEs. Examples would be delivery of basic services, conduct of manufacturing and agricultural activities, and transportation. The key to replicating the OE is resources. The level of fidelity and number of variables and subvariables replicated will be determined by factors such as the experience level of the unit, the type of training exercise, and the number of personnel available to role-play as members of an environment. Variables and their associated subvariables make the OE into an ever-changing and evolving situation that gives the training unit indications of upcoming and possible key events and reacts to actions the training unit takes or fails to take.

KEY EVENTS

2-79. Key events are preprogrammed events designed to highlight chosen training objectives. Early in the initial planning phase when the prioritized training objectives are developed, the senior trainer and exercise director usually determine if there will be key events and what their content will be. Key events found in exercises can involve things such as riots, mass casualties, and missing Soldiers.

2-80. To make the exercise more realistic and challenging, the exercise planner should consider key events more in terms of their relationship to the overall scenario, their training value, and their application across all PMESII-PT variables. Key events should also be precipitated by the buildup of indicators or situations that lead up to a key event. How the training unit responds to these indicators and events will determine the follow-on development of second-, third-, and even fourth-order effects. The training unit's reactions should be mapped out ahead of time and future events anticipated for scripting or role-playing instructions. The results can then be used as part of after action-reviews to show the training unit why something happened and what could have been done differently.

2-81. An example of key event development could involve an insurgency. In this example, the insurgency is part of training scenario and the unit's training objective of conducting stability operations. In this illustration, the exercise OE indicates an active insurgency in the vicinity of an important industrial city. This city also has an active black market and criminal activity. The planned key event would be the arrest of a suspected insurgent as the result of a raid on a meeting between leaders of this insurgency. Subsequent interrogations reveal that the person arrested is also the mayor of this city, a factory owner, and a tribal elder. How the training unit responds to this information will determine what and how the follow-on effects will play out. If the unit determines that he was only a sympathizer attending the meeting to placate the insurgency leaders, then the impacts of this arrest will be minimal. However, if the unit determines that he is lying and keeps him in detention without clear disposition, then the exercise director may cause a cascading of negative effects to develop. These effects may take place simultaneously and impact various PMESII-PT variables of this OE. Negative effects in this city may include: attitudes toward the U.S. forces, reduced local government effectiveness, factory shutdown, government strikes, demonstrations, riots, and increased criminal activity. These effects have already been predetermined and planned out to occur at certain times during the exercise unless the training unit takes actions to prevent or mitigate these effects. The sequence and level of resolution will most likely be based on the allocated time for the exercise and the unit's level of experience.

PRODUCTS

2-82. FM 7-0 states: "The Army trains and educates its members to develop agile leaders and organizations able to operate successfully in any operational environment." In order to achieve this goal, all leaders and trainers must understand not only what an OE is but its impact on the mission and training as well. Using all the eight PMESII-PT variables and the OE-WFF analysis provides analytical tools that help ensure comprehensive training objectives have been developed for the exercise. The resulting products from these tools are a defined OE as well as refined training objectives and task organization.

SECTION IV - PHASE 4: ORDERS, PLANS, AND INSTRUCTION DEVELOPMENT

2-83. Orders, plans, and instruction development refers to all the materials and products issued by the exercise director and his staff to the training unit. Normally this includes operation orders, operation plans (OPLANs), overlays, warning orders (WARNOs), fragmentary orders (FRAGOs), country studies, intelligence estimates, and adjacent unit orders—in short, all documents required for the training unit to exercise its staff and Soldiers during the exercise. Issue times for these orders vary, and the exercise planner should develop an orders issue schedule affording adequate lead times for training units to prepare and issue their orders. This schedule, as well as the documents themselves prior to their issue, may require changes and updates and should be reviewed and updated throughout the exercise.

2-84. There are three sets of orders and instructions derived from the exercise design process: training unit orders, OPFOR orders, and role-player instructions. These three sets of orders, while they may be developed separately, must be thoroughly coordinated before and during development. The exercise planner develops the orders, plans and instructions, which include the training unit's and OPFOR COAs, OPFOR OB, and the road to war.

TOOLS

2-85. Tools necessary for orders, plans, and instruction development are the results of phases 1 through 3 and the TC 7-100 series. Now that the OE is defined, the exercise planner can develop or refine the OPFOR OB to meet the requirements of the defined OE and then develop the training unit's higher headquarters order with COAs and finally the road to war.

2-86. As discussed earlier, the development of the OPFOR OB may have already occurred as part of phase 2 or phase 3, if the OE and OPFOR are already determined and at sufficient resolution for the training exercise requirements. If this is the case, then these tools, as well as others previously covered, would be used to develop OPFOR orders.

2-87. If the OPFOR OB has not been developed, then that process and OPFOR task-organizing would have to be completed during this phase since it is vital prerequisite data necessary for the production of OPFOR orders. For details on the development of OPFOR OB see phase 2, task and countertask development.

2-88. At this point, assuming OPFOR OB already exists, the exercise planner has established a number of the key conditions that allow him to begin positioning the training unit and OPFOR in tentative positions for start of exercise (STARTEX). He has determined how the exercise will flow, the order of the missions, and OB for both the training unit and OPFOR. The exercise planner should position OPFOR units in a way that provides sufficient combat power and types of forces to rigorously oppose the training unit and its performance of the training tasks. The exercise planner should organize the battlefield that—

- Provides nonlinear conditions.
- Reflects current Army and OPFOR doctrine.
- Is appropriate to the training unit troop list, training status, and AO.
- Matches the PMESII-PT variables and subvariable settings.

2-89. The exercise planner should then organize an OPFOR force that—

- Can accomplish all countertasks.
- Reflects TC 7-100-series OPFOR doctrine, organization, and equipment tier structure.
- Is appropriate to the training unit troop list and AO.
- Matches the appropriate PMESII-PT subvariable settings for Military.

2-90. During this phase, the training unit's higher headquarters COA is determined. The training unit's higher headquarters COA is determined largely by tools discussed earlier, such as the prioritized training objectives of unit to be trained. However, both the training unit and OPFOR COAs will affect and be affected by conditions (operational variables) pertinent to the exercise. In all cases, the exercise planner tries to find the best fit of conditions and parameters to support the scenario and training objectives. (For details on COA development, see FM 5-0.)

KEY DECISIONS

2-91. The final planning conference (also known as the STARTEX conference) between the exercise planner, exercise control (EXCON), OPFOR commander, senior trainer, and the exercise director is normally conducted during this phase in order to ensure all exercise details have been completed. The final planning conference or STARTEX conference locks in all troop lists, training objectives, and exercise conditions. This includes approval/disapproval by the exercise director of training unit requests for equipment and troop list exceptions outside of their normal TOE and task organization.

2-92. Approximately 30 days prior to STARTEX, the exercise planner prepares and presents the last pre-exercise briefing to the exercise director and all pertinent staff. Since this is designed as an information briefing, no decisions, except for unresolved issues, are expected from the exercise director. This briefing normally covers all aspects of the exercise and ensures deconfliction of any last-minute issues. It also promotes complete understanding of the exercise by those who are normally not part of the planning process. Topics covered in this briefing may include but are not limited to—

- Finalized troop list.
- Approved/disapproved equipment and troop list exceptions.
- Observer-controller augmentation (when required).
- Key leaders.
- Resolved and unresolved issues.
- Close air support/airlift units and sorties (if applicable).
- Detailed exercise timeline.
- Training unit missions and dispositions.
- OPFOR missions and dispositions.
- Chronology of major key events.
- CBRN events (if applicable).
- C-Day, M-Day, and D-Day.

PRODUCTS

2-93. To promote realism in training and to provide as much information as possible to the training unit prior to the exercise, the exercise director may direct the development and issuance of appropriate country studies, WARNOs, intelligence summaries, role-player instructions, and higher unit OPLANs. Training units may use these documents in developing preparatory home-station training prior to the actual exercise.

2-94. To this point, within the sequence of events, the exercise planner has compiled and developed all required information derived from his analysis of tools, key decisions, and products of the previous three phases. He has established and defined the key conditions for the OE and the exercise. He has also developed and analyzed COAs for both the training unit and OPFOR. The exercise planner is now prepared to expand the above-listed information into the orders and plans necessary to support the exercise.

HIGHER UNIT ORDERS AND PLANS

2-95. The number and detail of completeness of the orders and plans must be sufficient to meet all exercise requirements for the unit to be trained. Figure 2-4 is a list of typically required training-unit-associated orders and plans based on the level and fidelity of the exercise.

• Battalion WARNO	• COCOM WARNO
• Battalion OPORD	• Corps/Joint Task Force OPLAN
• Battalion FRAGO	
• Brigade WARNO	• Corps/Joint Task Force OPORD
• Brigade OPORD	
• Brigade FRAGO	• Country Studies
• Division WARNO	• Rules of Engagement
• Division OPORD	
• Division OPLAN	
• Division Intel Estimate	

Figure 2-4. Example of required orders and plans

OPFOR ORDERS AND PLANS

2-96. The OPFOR also uses plans and orders. OPFOR orders give specific guidance for exercise play and rules of engagement. Similar to the regular five-paragraph order format as described in FM 5-0, they may include special instructions for scripted events, as in the case of MRXs. Length, format, and detail will vary depending on the type of exercise, training area, and OPFOR organization. OPFOR orders and plans require careful husbanding by EXCON and the exercise director to ensure maintenance of control measures, rules of engagement, and force ratios in support of the exercise training requirements. Larger exercises require continuous exercise director review and modification to ensure fairness and proper observer-controller evaluation of the training unit.

2-97. OPFOR orders should, at a minimum, include—

- A description of the OE to include subvariable settings.
- A discussion of the scenario, a scenario timeline, areas to be occupied (who, what, where, when, and duration).
- Current higher-headquarters and strategic situation (OPFOR/training unit) and road to war.
- Task organization.
- Concept of operations to include coordinating instructions.
- Administrative notes.
- Events calendar/timetable.
- Rules of engagement (may be time- and unit-specific).
- Overlays and maps (for example, maneuver, fires, obstacle, reconnaissance and surveillance).
- Scripted events and coordination instructions when required (for example, MRXs, role-play interaction).

ROLE-PLAYER INSTRUCTIONS

2-98. Other written instructions that are important to develop during this phase are role-player instructions. Most exercise venues, including simulations, require interaction between the training unit and noncombatants. Role-player instructions create behavior profiles and events for individuals and groups within the role-player population. They also schedule specific events or incidents, which require close coordination between OPFOR, role-players, and EXCON.

2-99. Increasingly, training in civil affairs operations, the handling of news media, interaction with civilians (such as displaced persons, refugees and local inhabitants), as well as nongovernmental organizations (NGOs) has made the PMESII-PT Social and Political variables of primary concern to the exercise planner. The proliferation of transnational groups, criminal organizations, and international partnerships with U.S. and foreign companies has made OEs increasingly complex. Significant resources and coordination are required, depending on the exercise scenario, to script and execute desired incidents and events during exercises. Creative and tactically focused role-playing depicts the OE as a whole. Role-playing places training units in situations out of their comfort zone and forces them to make difficult decisions. It is a cornerstone of valuable training in today's training environments. Role-player instruction development, therefore, is a challenge for all exercise planners. For a detailed guide on the use of role-players in training, refer to the *Contemporary Operational Environment (COE) Actors & Role-Players Handbook*. It can be accessed on the TRISA-CTID website at https://www.us.army.mil/suite/files/14712167 (requires AKO password).

2-100. The *COE Actors & Role-Players Handbook* outlines a methodology for the orientation and training of role-players in COE-based education and training exercises. Each of the chapters contains specific information designed to assist exercise planners, exercise directors, and role-players in developing a realistic and challenging OE. The chapters include the following:

- Introduction to the COE.
- Role-player terminology.
- Individual and collective training considerations.
- Tools for trainers.

- Material and outfitting for the role-player.
- Media affairs and the role-player.
- Training program concept.

Figure 2-5 shows an example of the types of role-players described in the handbook.

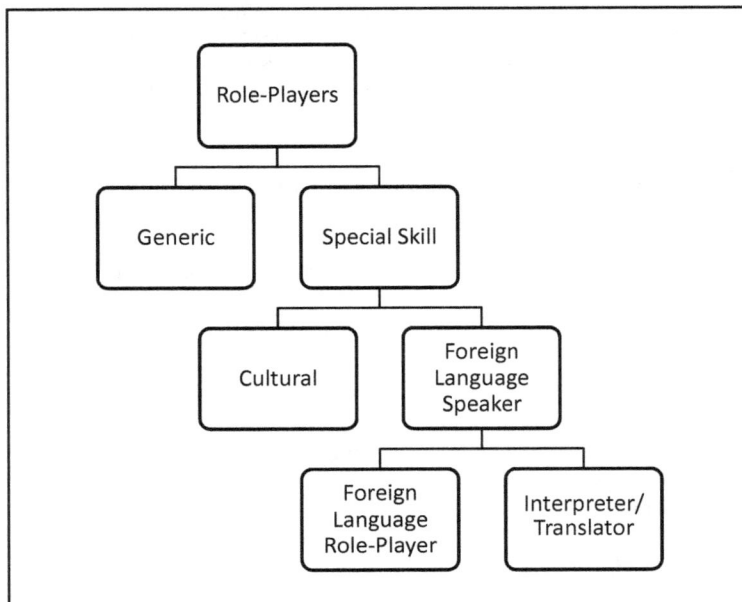

Figure 2-5. Types of role players

2-101. In order to support all training objectives and, ultimately, mission accomplishment, trainers must discuss key aspects of the OE for the exercise with role-players. By doing this, trainers ensure that role-players understand their functions and how they will provide the environment that enables the unit to meet its training objectives. Role-play instructions should include at a minimum the following information about the training unit:

- METL.
- Training objectives.
- Combined arms training strategy (CATS).
- Individual tasks and collective tasks.
- Battle tasks.
- Warrior tasks.

2-102. According to the *COE Actors & Role Players Handbook*, the exercise planner, trainers, and role-players must analyze all aspects of the scenario to ensure scenario fidelity. Role-players must be familiar with the—

- PMESII-PT variables and the training unit's desired subvariable settings.
- Training objectives.
- Role-player dynamics.
- Factors affecting the scenario.
- Scenario end state.

2-103.   A comprehensive list of role-player instructions is contained in the role-players handbook. Typical role-player instructions will—

- Force the training unit to interact with local officials and law enforcement.
- Cause situations that will test or force modification of the training unit's rules of engagement.
- Create situations that could cause possible violations of the rules of engagement and force the training unit to initiate investigations of alleged violations (AR 15-6).
- Stress the training unit's capabilities to deal with external organizations.
- Force the training unit's commander to deal with complaints regarding alleged injuries or deaths to civilians, destruction of civilian property, and failure to support NGO operations.
- Coordinate OPFOR interaction with civilians to cause unrest and depict the training unit as the enemy.
- Create an OE that forces the training unit to consider and plan for interaction with multiple external organizations.
- Introduce a number of third-party actors into exercise play.

ROAD TO WAR

2-104.   The last step in the exercise design process is to develop the road to war. The road to war is not necessarily a formal document but describes chronologically the incidents and the events leading up to the current situation as well as the training unit and OPFOR disposition. The road to war should be consistent with the subvariable settings selected for the OE variables. The road to war at a minimum should include the following:

- Explain the deployment and disposition of the training unit at STARTEX.
- Identify C-Day, M-Day, and D-Day.
- Explain OPFOR organization of the battlefield, organization of forces, and dispositions.
- Reflect OPFOR doctrine in the TC 7-100 series (except for MRXs).
- Provide reasoning for execution of training objectives and subtasks.

SECTION V - SUMMARY

2-105.   The planning events discussed in this chapter represent a practical approach to developing and executing training exercises. The events discussed provide context to exercise design and scenario development. Still, exact events and timings will be prescribed by each training organization, such as MCTC or Battle Command Training Program (BCTP).

2-106.   Exercise design is an integrated process involving the determination of exercise parameters (phase 1, initial planning), development of training tasks (phase 2, task and countertask development), design of exercise conditions (phase 3, PMESII-PT OE development), and orders production (phase 4, orders, plans, and instruction development). These four phases meld the basic exercise design steps with the eight operational variables of PMESII-PT and their subvariable settings. This process, while extensive, ensures exercise continuity and compliance with the COE concept and OPFOR doctrine in the TC 7-100 series. A composite checklist with exercise development tasks and critical planning events can be found in appendix A.

This page intentionally left blank.

Chapter 3
Operational Variables

As discussed in chapter 2, the operational variables provide key design considerations for the exercise planner. Together, these variables comprise all the conditions, circumstances, and influences that affect any military operation or any training exercise. They provide a comprehensive view of an operational environment (OE), real or simulated, that realistically challenges the training unit, its leaders, and Soldiers in the execution of their missions and tasks. This chapter describes the variables, subvariables, and linkages that can be used to develop comprehensive OE conditions for training exercises.

OPERATIONAL ENVIRONMENT

3-1. An OE is the complete set of conditions, circumstances, and influences that affect the decisions of the unit commander and the deployment and employment of military forces, as well as other instruments of national power. It encompasses all the variables that affect where Soldiers will train or fight.

3-2. The OE represented in a training event must be appropriate for the training objectives. What constitutes a realistic and relevant OE for a particular training event depends on how much the unit knows about where it can expect to be deployed. On the one hand, the unit may know the specific area of operations (AO) where it will deploy or be able to anticipate such a specific deployment. In that case, the goal should be to create training conditions that replicate as closely as possible the actual conditions of the specific OE associated with that AO. On the other hand, the unit may need to train to accomplish its core capabilities in any of a number of possible OEs. In that case, it is appropriate to design an OE that represents a composite of the types of conditions that might exist in a number of actual OEs in which the unit might find itself involved in full spectrum operations.

3-3. In either case, the design and structure of the OE for any training event consists of three main components: actual data, projected data, and intelligent compromise. All that differs is the proportion of each. The term for this combination of actual data, intelligent compromise, and projected information that creates the conditions for any training event is the **Contemporary Operational Environment (COE). The COE is the collective set of conditions, derived from a composite of actual worldwide conditions, that pose realistic challenges for training, leader development, and capabilities development for Army forces and their joint, intergovernmental, interagency and multinational partners.** The COE is a collective term for the relevant aspects of contemporary OEs that exist or could exist today or in the, near- and mid-term future (next 10 years). It is a composite of all the **operational variables** and **actors** that create the conditions, circumstances, and influence that can affect military operations—and therefore serve as the conditions necessary for training and leader development. Most importantly, it is not a totally artificial construct created for training; rather, it is a representative composite based on the characteristics of one or more actual OEs in this contemporary timeframe.

VARIABLES, SUBVARIABLES, AND SETTINGS

3-4. The foundation of the exercise planner's development of the appropriate OE for a training exercise is the eight operational variables that reside in all OEs and have the greatest impact on military forces. The strength of these variables is that they are flexible and scalable, capable of replicating any OE that U.S. forces might encounter along the full spectrum of conflict. These variables are Political, Military, Economic, Social, Information, Infrastructure, Physical Environment, and Time (PMESII-PT). The variables relate to specific situations as well as threat capabilities. They are relevant to every echelon of command and every military mission. While individual variables do not dominate every environment, they are all present and require careful consideration. Ignoring one or more of these variables can negatively impact military missions and the realism of training conditions in an exercise.

3-5. The taxonomy of categorizing the components of any OE begins with the eight PMESII-PT. The next level down from the variables is the associated subvariables, which show either a menu or a range of choices called subvariable settings. In a few cases, a subvariable may break down into another level of specificity, called *sub-subvariables*, which have their own choices of settings. Each variable, associated subvariables and sub-subvariables, and their settings have specific definitions to assist the planner in building the desired OE.

> *Note.* The listed subvariables and associated settings are not necessarily all inclusive. As events, technology, and time change, existing subvariables may need to be modified or new ones added. Even in conducting an operational environment assessment (OEA) for an actual OE, additional subvariables may be necessary. The intent in this TC is to provide a basic guideline of areas that are important and may need to be considered in designing a training exercise.

3-6. The remaining portion of this chapter will provide a detailed breakdown of each operational variable and their associated components in the order of the memory aid PMESII-PT. The entry for each variable begins with the definition of that variable. Then, for each variable, there is an initial table providing an overview of the associated subvariables and subvariable settings. This is followed by individual tables for each subvariable, providing the subvariable definition and definitions of possible subvariable settings. The subvariable tables also include "considerations and additional notes" usually pertaining to individual settings. Finally, the subvariable tables list other variables and subvariables whose settings would most likely be linked to the subvariable described in the table. However, these are not the only possible links that may exist.

3-7. Exercise planners should use these tables as a tool to select the subvariable or sub-subvariable settings that create the appropriate conditions for their specific exercise. These specific conditions, along with scenarios and road to war, are based upon approved training objectives, the training unit's METL, and desired exercise-training outcomes. When training for an actual OE in a specific geographical area, the exercise planner can use a TRISA-produced OEA that indicates the settings required to replicate that particular OE (see chapter 2).

3-8. The impacts of the PMESII-PT variables on exercise design are significant. As discussed in chapter 2, the PMESII-PT variables and their subvariable and sub-subvariable settings provide a comprehensive framework to determine the training conditions within an OE. These conditions can affect the training unit and OPFOR positively and negatively across the full spectrum of operations as well as at the strategic, operational, and tactical levels. Using these variables assists the commander in training his unit in a realistic and challenging environment.

POLITICAL VARIABLE

3-9. The Political variable describes the distribution of responsibility and power at all levels of governance—formally constituted authorities, as well as informal political powers. The political variable includes influential political groups and the collective attitude of the population towards the U.S. The specific Political subvariables and their settings are depicted in table 3-1. Their associated definitions, considerations, additional notes, and external links are listed separately in tables 3-2 through 3-6.

Table 3-1. Political variable and subvariable settings

Variable	Political				
Subvariable	Attitude toward the United States	Centers of Political Power	Type of Government	Government Effectiveness and Legitimacy	Influential Political Groups
Subvariable Settings	Friendly	Tribal	Dictatorship/ Authoritarian	Effective: Stable	Pro-Government
	Neutral/ Ambivalent	Town/District	Theocracy	Vulnerable: Recovering	Opposition
	Hostile	Provincial	Representative Government	Vulnerable: Failing	Coalition
		National/ Regional	Anarchy	Crisis: Failing	
				Crisis: Failed	

Table 3-2. Political: attitude toward the United States

Definition: Describes the attitude of the government toward the United States and specifically toward the presence and actions of U.S. and/or coalition forces. (Once established, this subvariable manifests itself in the scenario in the form of role player instructions or combat instructions to the OPFOR.)		
Subvariable Setting	**Setting Definition**	**Considerations and Additional Notes**
Friendly	Describes an overall favorable, positive reception of the U.S. and/or coalition forces activities, presence, and initiatives.	Role-player sub-instructions limited to 20% of subversive activities against the training unit's intentions. Takes the form of infiltration, overlooking of criminal activities, active support of OPFOR. Also necessitates 20% of role-player support in the form of tips. Limits infiltration and scripted sabotage against the training unit's actions. High level of tips (4 to 5 per day) and populace cooperation against OPFOR activities.
Neutral/Ambivalent	Describes an undecided reception of the U.S. and/or coalition forces' activities, presence, and initiatives.	Role-player sub-instructions limited to 30% of the scenario population engaged in some form of subversive activities against the training unit's intentions. Takes the form of infiltration, overlooking of criminal activities, and active support of OPFOR. Also necessitates 15% of role-player support in the form of tips. Increased infiltration and scripted sabotage against the training unit's actions. Moderate level of tips, (2 to 3 per day) and populace cooperation against OPFOR activities.
Hostile	Describes an unfavorable, negative reaction to the U.S. and/or coalition forces' activities, presence, and initiatives.	Role-player sub-instructions limited to 40% of the scenario population engaged in some form of subversive activities against the training unit's intentions. Takes the form of infiltration, overlooking of criminal activities, and active support of OPFOR. Heavy infiltration and scripted sabotage against the training unit's actions. Low level of tips (1 to 2 per day) and populace cooperation against OPFOR activities.
Subvariable Links: Political: Type of Government; Social: Education Level; Economic: Employment Status.		

Table 3-3. Political: centers of political power

Definition: Determines the types of bureaucratic divisions and/or centers of power within a government. Also includes the level of governmental span of control from tr bal to regional/national level. An example would be tribal and town/district, with a primary focus on town/district matters.

Subvariable Setting	Setting Definition	Considerations and Additional Notes
Tribal	Tribal focus, limited government or government of limited influence. Characterized by tribal elders, religious figureheads.	Requires tr bal elders, some town element manning, and portions of the other role-playing requirements element (such as NGOs, and host or allied nation military presence).
Town/District	Town and some district focus in the government day-to-day operations.	Requires district and town elements.
Provincial	Provincial and minimal cross-border focus by the local and provincial government.	Some regional (international) elements and story themes present in the scenario. Government role-players adopt a national focus at the expense of local and tribal needs. Depending upon the government type and status, up to one full role-player provincial government, district, town, and other group will be required to fully replicate the level of government specified.
National/Regional	International and cross-border focus based on the existence of multiple regions or national borders in the scenario OE.	Also requires provincial, district, town, other elements (manned at some level of capacity).

Subvariable Links: Political: Type of Government; Social: Education level, Ethnic Diversity: Infrastructure: Transportation.

Table 3-4. Political: type of government

Definition: Determines the type of government structure and associated behaviors encountered.

Subvariable Setting	Setting Definition	Considerations and Additional Notes
Dictatorship/Authoritarian	A mode of government characterized by the existence of a single ruler or group who arrogate to themselves and monopolize power in the state, exercising it without restraint.	For live training requires robust domestic security apparatus, bureaucratic institutions, and bloated role-player government structure (1.5 normal manning).
Theocracy	A government ruled by or subject to religious authority. A system of government in which God or a deity is held to be the civil ruler.	Can only occur in the first two categories of social religious diversity.
Representative Government	A representative form of government—either democratic, republic, or parliamentary in form—with elected representatives and executives. All politics are governed by will of people and government has limited, defined powers over the population.	Requires specific, prominent influencers, council members be present in the scenario (in addition to the normal role-player government positions).
Anarchy	Absence of any form of political authority. Political disorder and confusion. Absence of any cohesive principle, such as a common standard or purpose.	Tr bal and religious role-players present in scenario. Small percentage of disenfranchised or former government officials with little influence.

Subvariable Links: Economic: Illegal Economic Activity, Social: Education Level, Religious Diversity, Criminal Activity.

Table 3-5. Political: government effectiveness and legitimacy

Definition: *Effectiveness* refers to the capability of the government to work with society to assure the provision of order and public goods and services. *Legitimacy* refers to the perception by important segments of society that the government is exercising state power in ways that are reasonably fair and in the interests of the nation as a whole.

Subvariable Setting	Setting Definition	Considerations and Additional Notes
Effective: Stable	The government is able and willing to provide adequate security and essential services to significant portions of its country's population. It provides military and police services that secure borders and limit crime, while being reasonable, equitable, and without major violation of human rights. It provides basic services that generally meet demand. Political institutions, processes, norms, and leaders are acceptable to the citizenry and ensure adequate response to citizen needs.	For CTC replication, full complement of all specified role-player government positions required in the provincial, district and town elements. Government manning determined by the type of government selected. Defined as 60-75% of all government services provided throughout the OE, 60-75% of all infrastructures present and functioning. Limited civil unrest. Limited governance issues and themes (no more than three). 1-2 instances of civil unrest or riots as a result of those issues and themes.
Vulnerable: Recovering	The government is recovering from crisis and still either unable or unwilling to provide adequate security and essential services to all of the population. The legitimacy of the central government may still be in question. Limited civil unrest.	The government is only partially manned and capable of administering its area. For CTC replication, requires 3/4 complement of all specified role-player government positions within the OE. Defined as 40-60% of all government services provided throughout the OE, 60-75% of all infrastructures present and functioning. Moderate governance issues and themes (4-6, 2 of which are interrelated). Multiple (3-4) instances of civil unrest or riots as a result of those issues and themes.
Vulnerable: Failing	The government is becoming either unable or unwilling to provide adequate security and essential services to significant portions of the population. The legitimacy of the central government is falling into question. Increasing civil unrest.	The government is only partially manned and capable of administering its area. For CTC replication, requires 3/4 complement of all specified role-player government positions within the OE. Defined as 40-60% of all government services provided throughout the OE, 60-75% of all infrastructures present and functioning. Moderate governance issues and themes (4-6, 2 of which are interrelated). Multiple (3-4) instances of civil unrest or riots as a result of those issues and themes.
Crisis: Failing	The central government does not exert effective control over all the country's territory. It is becoming unable or unwilling to provide security and essential services for significant portions of the population. The central government may be weak, nonexistent, or simply unable or unwilling to provide security or basic services. There is great risk of violent internal conflict.	The government is partially manned and minimally capable of administering its area. For CTC replication requires 1/2 or fewer complement of all specified role-player government positions within the OE. Defined as 20-40% of all government services provided throughout the OE, 60-75% of all infrastructures present and functioning. High level of governance issues and themes (8-10, 4 of which are interrelated). Multiple (5-6) instances of civil unrest or riots as a result of those issues and themes.
Crisis: Failed	The central government does not exert effective control over the country's territory. It is unable to provide security and essential services for significant portions of the population. The central government is weak, nonexistent, or simply unable to provide security or basic services. Violent internal conflict is a reality.	The government is partially manned and largely incapable of administering its area. For CTC replication requires 1/4 or fewer complement of all specified role-player government positions within the OE. Defined as 20-40% of all government services provided throughout the OE, 60-75% of all infrastructures present and functioning. High level of governance issues and themes (8-10, 4 of which are interrelated). Multiple (5-6) instances of civil unrest or riots as a result of those issues and themes.

Subvariable Links: Political: Governance, Stability; Infrastructure: Utilities Present, Services Level.

Table 3-6. Political: influential political groups

Definition: Describes the number and specifies the interaction and influence of various political groups within the country, region, province, district, or town. Helps define the level of government cohesion and strife within the government.

Subvariable Setting	Setting Definition	Considerations and Additional Notes
Pro-Government	Major political parties generally support the government in power. Minimal dissent and issues of contention.	Presented and manifested in OE through scripting and role-player sub-instructions. If desired, minor issues may result in slight disruption of essential government functions if unaddressed or not resolved by the training unit.
Coalitions	Different political groups with competing interests and vary in their support of the government. Establishes conditions for moderate disruption of essential government functions and social volatility.	Requires the establishment of up to three different political groups with at least two competing interests to be written into the scenario key events, back-stories, and role-player sub-instructions. Conflicts should be executed or presented during the training exercise, using power bases and role-player influencers. Issues should result in the moderate disruption of essential government functions if unaddressed or not resolved by the training unit.
Opposition	Different political groups are opposed to the government with competing interests. Establishes conditions for major disruption of essential government functions and social volatility.	Requires the establishment of up to three different political groups with at least two competing interests to be written into the scenario key events, back-stories, and role-player sub-instructions. Conflicts should be executed or presented during the training exercise, using power bases and role-player influencers. Issues should result in the major disruption of essential government functions if unaddressed or not resolved by the training unit.

Subvariable Links: Social: Social Volatility, Education Level; Economic: Economic Diversity, Employment Status.

MILITARY VARIABLE

3-10. The Military variable explores the military and/or paramilitary capabilities of all relevant actors (enemy, friendly, and neutral) in a given OE. This includes nonmilitary armed and unarmed combatants. The variable focuses on giving the exercise planner the ability to design appropriate OPFOR units for full spectrum operations. The specific military subvariables and their settings are depicted in table 3-7. Their associated definitions, considerations, additional notes, and external links are listed separately in tables 3-8 through 3-13.

Table 3-7. Military variable and subvariable settings

Variable	Military					
Subvariable	Military Forces	Government Military Forces	Non-State Paramilitary Forces	Unarmed Comba-tants	Nonmilitary Armed Combatants	Military Functions
Subvariable Settings	Predominantly Tank and Mechanized Infantry	Operating Independently	Insurgent Forces	Information Warfare Personnel	Predominantly Neutral	C2
	Predominantly Infantry	Supplementing Regular Military	Guerrilla Forces	Media (Affiliated)	Predominantly Friendly	Maneuver
	None	Operating as Combat Forces	Criminal Organizations	Medical (Affiliated)	Predominantly Hostile and Supporting Enemy	Information Warfare
			Private Security Organizations	Active Sup-porters	Undetermined	RISTA
				Coerced or Unwitting		Fire Support
				Financiers		Protection
				See complete settings at table 3-11.		Logistics

Table 3-8. Military: military forces

Definition: Specifies the types and sizes of military forces present within an OE.		
Subvariable Settings	Setting Definition	Considerations and Additional Notes
Predominantly Tank and Mechanized Infantry	Regular military forces consisting predominantly (at least 40%) of tank and mechanized infantry forces with some infantry (non-mechanized).	For specific tier level weapon systems, refer to *Worldwide Equipment Guide* (WEG) available online at https://www.us.army.mil/suite/files/14751393.
Predominantly Infantry	Regular military forces consisting predominantly (more than 60%) of infantry forces (non-mechanized) with some tank and mechanized infantry forces.	
None	No regular military forces present.	
Subvariable Links: Social: Education Level; Economic: Employment Status; Terrain: Landforms.		

Table 3-9. Military: government paramilitary forces

Definition: Descr bes government forces that are distinct from regular armed forces, but resembling them in organization, training, or mission.

Subvariable Settings	Setting Definition	Considerations and Additional Notes
Operating Independently	Not subordinate to or affiliated with regular military forces.	May include organizations such as police, border guards, customs agents, and other internal security forces.
Supplementing Regular Military	Affiliated with or subordinate to regular military forces but performing primarily non-combat roles.	Same as above with the exception that these forces are either part of the military force or can be mobilized to support the military force.
Operating as Combat Forces	Affiliated with or subordinate to regular military forces and performing combat missions. (Units are equipped with light weapons and sometimes heavy weapons and armored vehicles.)	Same as above with the exception that these forces are trained and equipped for combat missions. Depending on the OE, they may be equipped with light or heavy weapon systems.

Subvariable Links: Military: Non-State Paramilitary Forces; Economic: Employment Status.

Table 3-10. Military: non-state paramilitary forces

Definition: Descr bes forces or groups that are distinct from regular armed forces of any country, but resembling them in organization, training, or mission (JP 1-02 and FM 3-07). These forces or groups may also operate in a combination of two or more of the subvariable settings below. (Not government forces.)

Subvariable Settings	Setting Definition	Considerations and Additional Notes
Insurgent Forces	An *insurgency* is an organized movement aimed at the overthrow of a constituted government through use of subversion and armed conflict. (JP 3-05) *Insurgent forces* are groups that conduct irregular or unconventional warfare within the borders of their country in order to undermine or overthrow a constituted government or civil authority.	The distinction between terrorists and insurgents is often blurred because of the tactics employed by each. Some terrorists groups have become insurgent organizations, while insurgent organizations have used terror tactics. An insurgent organization may use more than one form of tactics and, based on its strategy, its actions could cut across the entire spectrum of warfare—employing terror, guerrilla, and conventional military tactics to achieve its goals. Typically, most insurgent groups use the first two.
Guerrilla Forces	A *guerrilla force* is a group of irregular, predominantly indigenous personnel organized along military lines to conduct military and paramilitary operations in enemy-held, hostile, or denied territory. (JP 3-05)	Some guerrilla organizations may constitute a paramilitary arm of an insurgent movement, while others may pursue guerrilla warfare independently from or loosely affiliated with an insurgent organization. Compared to insurgent organizations as a whole, guerrilla organizations have a more military-l ke structure. (FM 7-100.4)
Criminal Organizations	Criminal organizations are non-ideological groups of people organized for the purpose of acquiring money by illegal means.	Criminal organizations may employ criminal actions, terror tactics, and militarily unconventional methods to achieve their goals. When mutual interests exist, criminal organizations may combine efforts with insurgent and/or guerrilla organizations controlling or operating in the same area. A congruence of interests can also result in criminal organizations having a close relationship with an established government. (FM 7-100.4)

(continued)

Table 3-10. Military: non-state paramilitary forces (continued)

Subvariable Settings	Setting Definition	Considerations and Additional Notes
Private Security Organizations	Private security organizations (PSOs) are business enterprises or local ad hoc groups that provide security and/or intelligence services, on a contractual or self-interest basis, to protect and preserve a person, facility, or operation. (FM 7-100.4).	A PSO sometimes acts as an adjunct to other security measures, and provides advisors, instruction, and personnel for host-nation military, paramilitary, and police forces, as well as for private individuals and businesses (including transnational corporations).
Subvariable Links: Political: Government Effectiveness and Legitimacy; Social: Education Level; Economic: Economic Activity.		

Table 3-11. Military: unarmed combatants

Definition: Specifies the types of unarmed personnel who, given the right conditions, may decide to purposely and materially support hostile military or paramilitary forces in ways that do not involve possessing or using weapons. Even unarmed individuals who are coerced into performing or supporting hostile actions and those who do so unwittingly can, in some cases, be categorized as combatants. (FM 7-100.4)

Subvariable Settings	Setting Definition	Considerations and Additional Notes
Information Warfare Personnel	Self-explanatory.	The intent of this subvariable is to provide a menu list from which to select those personnel or activities that provide direct or indirect support to an insurgency or similar activity. Providing these selected settings as part of an insurgency in an OE enhances a unit's training by experiencing a more complete, realistic, and complex environment.
Media (Affiliated)	Self-explanatory.	
Medical (Affiliated)	Self-explanatory.	
Active Supporters	Self-explanatory.	
Coerced, Unwitting Supporters	Self-explanatory.	
Financiers	Self-explanatory.	
Suppliers	Self-explanatory.	
Lookouts	Self-explanatory.	
Couriers	Self-explanatory.	
IED Factory Workers	Self-explanatory.	
Intelligence Collection	Self-explanatory.	
Targeting Information	Self-explanatory.	
Leaders (Religious, Political, Secular, Tribal, Cultural)	Self-explanatory.	
Technicians and Specialists	Self-explanatory.	
Criminal (Affiliated)	Self-explanatory.	
Transporters	Self-explanatory.	
Asylum Providers/Protectors	Self-explanatory.	
Recruiters	Self-explanatory.	
Camera/Video Operators	Self-explanatory.	
IED Trigger Personnel	Self-explanatory.	
Other Affiliated Support	Self-explanatory.	
None	No unarmed combatants present.	
Subvariable Links: Political: Attitude toward the United States; Economic: Economic Activity; Military: Non-State Paramilitary Forces, Military Functions.		

Table 3-12. Military: nonmilitary armed combatants

Definition: Descr bes nonmilitary personnel who are armed but not part of an organized paramilitary or military structure. Nevertheless, they may be disgruntled and hostile. They may also be neutral or they may support either the enemy or friend-ly (U.S. or host nation) forces. Any number of catalysts might cause them to pick a side or change sides. Their decision may or may not remain permanent. (FM 7-100.4)

Subvariable Settings	Setting Definition	Considerations and Additional Notes
Predominantly Neutral	At least 50 percent neutral, with the remainder split between friendly, hostile, or undetermined.	
Predominantly Friendly	At least 50 percent friendly to U.S. or host nation forces, with the remainder split between neutral, hostile, or undetermined.	
Predominantly Hostile and Support-ing Enemy	At least 50 percent hostile to U.S. or host nation forces or supporting the enemy, with the remainder split between neutral, friendly, or undetermined.	
Undetermined	Unable to categorize relationship.	This setting may be used to support training objectives related to determining or responding correctly to nonmilitary armed combatants whose affiliation is unknown.

Subvariable Links: Military: Unarmed Combatants; Social: Education Level; Economic: Economic Status.

Table 3-13. Military: military functions

Definition: A *military function* is a group of related tasks, activities, capabilities, operations, processes, and organizations that fulfill the specific military purpose for which they all exist. When integrated with other such functions, they contribute to the accomplishment of larger missions.

The subvariable settings (functions) listed below exist in varying degrees in most military organizations, as well as in some paramilitary organizations. Thus, military functions as sub-subvariables can have settings on a scale of High, Medium, or Low, defined as follows:

- *High*: Can conduct sustained, complex, synchronized tasks of the selected military function; ability to influence friendly forces is not limited to the theater of operations; and/or associated equipment is predominantly Tier 1, as specified in the *Worldwide Equipment Guide* (WEG).
- *Medium*: Can conduct limited, complex, synchronized tasks of the selected military function; ability to influence friendly forces is primarily limited to the theater of operations; and/or associated equipment is predominantly Tier 2, as specified in the WEG.
- *Low*: Cannot conduct complex, synchronized tasks of the selected military function; ability to influence friendly forces is limited to local, tactical impact; and/or associated equipment is predominantly Tier 3 and below, as specified in the WEG.

Subvariable Setting	Setting Definition	Considerations and Additional Notes
Command and Control	*Command and control* (C2) is the actions of commanders, command groups, and staffs of military headquarters to maintain continual combat readiness and combat efficiency of forces, to plan and prepare for combat operations, and to provide leadership and direction during the execution of assigned missions. (FM 7-100.1)	
Maneuver	*Maneuver* is the employment of forces in the operational area through movement in combination with fires to achieve a position of advantage in respect to the enemy in order to accomplish the mission. (JP 3-0) This function includes direct fire, as well as mobility support and countermobility operations.	
INFOWAR	*Information warfare* (INFOWAR) is the specifically planned and integrated actions taken to achieve an information advantage at critical points and times. (FM 7-100.1)	This function is linked to Information: Information Warfare, which addresses each of the seven elements of information warfare.

(continued)

Table 3-13. Military: military functions (continued)

Subvariable Setting	Setting Definition	Considerations and Additional Notes
RISTA	*Reconnaissance, intelligence, surveillance, and target acquisition* (RISTA) is the combination of capabilities, operations, and activities using all available means to obtain information concerning foreign nations; areas of actual or potential operations; and/or the strength, capabilities, location, status, nature of operations, and intentions of hostile or potentially hostile forces or elements. It includes production of intelligence resulting from the collection, processing, integration, evaluation, analysis, and interpretation of such information. It also includes detection, identification, and location of a target in sufficient detail to permit the effective employment of weapons.	RISTA includes UAVs used for reconnaissance. This function is linked to Information: Intelligence.
Fire Support	*Fire support* is the collective and coordinated use of target acquisition, indirect fire weapons, aircraft, and other lethal and nonlethal means in support of operational or tactical objectives. (FM 7-100.1)	Includes offensive use of CBRN weapons. This function is linked to the target acquisition portion of the RISTA function (above).
Protection	*Protection* is the preservation of the effectiveness and survivability of mission-related military and nonmilitary personnel (combatants and noncombatants), equipment, facilities, information, and infrastructure against an adversary's attempts to damage, degrade, or negate them and measures to minimize the effects of such threats. The protection function includes survivability measures, air and missile defense, and CBRN defense. It also includes information protection and security measures, which are an element of information warfare.	This function is linked to Information: Information Warfare: Protection and Security Measures and, therefore, to the Information Warfare setting under Military: Military Functions (above). It is also linked to Information Security as a subset of Information: Information Management and to the Infrastructure variable.
Logistics	*Logistics* is the support activities required to sustain operations. (FM 7-100.1)	
Subvariable Links: See notes on individual military functions, above.		

ECONOMIC VARIABLE

3-11. The Economic variable encompasses individual and group behaviors related to producing, distributing, and consuming resources. Specific factors impacting behavior may include economic diversity and employment opportunities within an OE. Other factors include black market or underground economies, which are alternative structures indicating weaknesses in the mainstream economy. Such factors influence people's decisions to alter or support the existing order. These decisions, if unresolved through legitimate political means, can lead to conflict. The specific economic subvariables and their settings represent replicable economic conditions that may be present within an OE and are depicted in table 3-14. Their associated definitions, considerations, additional notes, and external links are listed separately in tables 3-15 through 3-19.

Table 3-14. Economic variable and subvariable settings

Variable	Economic				
Subvariable	Economic Diversity	Employment Status	Economic Activity	Illegal Economic Activity	Banking and Finance
Subvariable Settings	Multiple Industries (None Predominant)	High Unemployment	Predominantly Legal	Smuggling	Informal
	Multiple Industries (Single Predominant)	Medium Unemployment	Mixed	Theft	Developing Formal
	Single Industry Present	Low Unemployment	Predominantly Illegal	Gang	Advanced Formal
				Black Market	
				Mixed	
				Piracy	

Table 3-15. Economic: economic diversity

Definition: Describes three different economic industries (mining, manufacturing, or agricultural) and their relative mix that may exist in a given country.		
Subvariable Settings	**Setting Definition**	**Considerations and Additional Notes**
Multiple Industries (None Predominant)	Describes the condition where multiple industries are present in an economy. All three industries are roughly equivalent in terms of their overall contribution to the overall economy.	For live training exercises, a series of props, role-player instructions and scripted activities are required that replicate a complete agriculture, mining, manufacturing infrastructure to include harvesting, processing, and distribution. Minimum material requirements include one barn, one grain silo, one planting field; one mineshaft and distribution site; one factory with one shop selling at least one specific product line and one distribution center.
Multiple Industries (Single Predominant)	Describes the condition where multiple industries are present in an economy but one of the industries is more productive relative to the others.	Same as above with the exception that the selected predominant industry will require at least twice the amount of props and role-players to replicate predominance in that nation's economy. Any single industry selected as predominant will cause exercise planners to ensure the preponderance of storylines, themes, and role-players are focused on that industry and all of its associated parts.

(continued)

Table 3-15. Economic: economic diversity (continued)

Subvariable Settings	Setting Definition	Considerations and Additional Notes
Single Industry Present	Describes the condition of a single, economically significant industry.	Same as above except that the selected predominant industry is the only one present and should also be at least twice the size of the multiple industry setting. The industry theme selected acts as the focal point for all economic storylines, themes, and role-players focused on that industry and its sustainment.
Subvariable Links: Economic: Employment Status; Social: Education Level; Infrastructure: Urban Zones, Transportation Architecture.		

Table 3-16. Economic: employment status

Definition: Represents the overall employment status of the populace.		
Subvariable Settings	Setting Definition	Considerations and Additional Notes
High Unemployment	2/3 unemployment.	For live training exercises it manifests itself in specific role assignments and sub-instructions for role-players.
Moderate Unemployment	1/2 unemployment.	
Low Unemployment	Majority employed.	
Subvariable Links: Economic: Economic Diversity; Social: Education Level; Political: Government Effectiveness and Legitimacy.		

Table 3-17. Economic: economic activity

Definition: Descr bes the type of economic activity present in an AO.		
(Manifests itself in a live training environment in the form of specific activities, number of role-players required to replicate the behavior, and scenario design instructions in the form of role descriptions for different activities.)		
Subvariable Setting	Setting Definition	Considerations and Additional Notes
Predominantly Illegal	Economy lacking many products and services; black market operations robbery, smuggling, and organized crime are widespread.	For live training exercises, it will require a role-player special mission element to replicate those conditions. Or will require sufficient role-player instructions and character instructions to replicate these activities. Black market and smuggling are represented by three or more types of illicit goods being traded—one or more necessary to population well being.
Mixed	Legal economy mixed with some smuggling and black market trade in controlled items.	Will require half role-player special mission element to replicate limited black market and some organized crime. Will also require at least two smuggling or black market trading themes written into the scenario storyline in the form of role-player instructions. Also requires government ministers and regulation (customs) ministries to regulate economy.
Predominantly Legal	Limited black market, robbery, or organized crime activities.	Types of crime replicated: petty theft and limited drug or single item smuggling, distribution and sales. Requires up to 2 role-player special mission elements worth of personnel to populate district markets and replicate regional trade and limited black market activity. Also requires government ministers and regulation (customs) ministries to regulate economy.
Subvariable Links: Political: Type of Government; Economic: Employment Status; Social: Education Level, Social Volatility.		

Table 3-18. Economic: illegal economic activity

Definition: Descr bes the predominant type of illegal economic activities present in the AO.		
Subvariable Setting	**Setting Definition**	**Considerations and Additional Notes**
Smuggling	The acquisition, distr bution, and sale of a con-trolled, restricted, or forbidden item.	Requires the replication of all aspects of the distribution chain, from suppliers to mules, to retail customers. For live training exercises, each activity represented requires 1/4 of the role-player special mission element to replicate the activity, and role-player instructions, in addi-tion to scenario storyline.
Theft/Looting	Small theft rings that acquire and distribute stolen property.	Same as above.
Gang/Organized Crime	Criminal activities such as br bery, coercion, thuggery, protection racket, and inter-gang riva-lry.	Same as above.
Black Market	The underground economy or black market is a market where all commerce is conducted with-out regard to taxation, law, or regulations of trade.	Same as above.
Piracy	Robbery, hijacking, or other acts of violence on the high seas. Can also include acts committed in other major bodies of water or on a shore.	Same as above.
Mixed/Multiple Activities	Multiple above-mentioned activities present in the AO.	Same as above in addition to representation by multiple key events occurring during the scena-rio play.
Subvariable Links: Political: Government Effectiveness and Legitimacy; Economic: Economic Activity, Social: Criminal Activity.		

Table 3-19. Economic: banking and finance

Definition: A bank is a financial institution whose primary activity is to act as a payment agent for customers and to borrow and lend money. It is an institution for receiving, keeping, and lending money in hopes of repayment. A private moneylender offers small personal loans at high rates of interest, usually higher rates than the market rate charged on credit cards or on bank overdrafts.		
Subvariable Setting	**Setting Definition**	**Considerations and Additional Notes**
Informal	A private moneylender type arrangement.	For live training exercises, currency require-ments are enough denominations of currency to issue 20 bills of various denominations to each role-player present in the AO. Requires at least one moneylender, with currency per town.
Developing-Formal	Mixture of private moneylenders and banking infrastructure.	Same as above. Also includes a bank building with props per town.
Advanced-Formal	Banking infrastructure prevalent throughout the AO. Private money lending restricted to crimi-nal/gang activity.	Same as above.
Subvariable Links: Political: Type of Government; Social: Education Level, Information: Public Communications Media.		

SOCIAL VARIABLE

3-12. The Social variable describes the cultural, religious, and ethnic makeup within an OE and the beliefs, values, customs, and behaviors of society members. Societies are comprised of structured and overlapping groups and institutions, each with relative statuses and roles that support, enable, and provide opportunity to achieve personal or community expectations. Important characteristics of a social system include population demographics, migration trends, and diversity of religious and ethnic groups. Understanding these complex interrelationships in a society is vitally important for successful military missions. The specific social subvariables and their settings represent replicable social conditions that may be present within an OE and are depicted in table 3-20. Their associated definitions, considerations, additional notes, and external links are listed separately in tables 3-21 through 3-29.

Table 3-20. Social variable and subvariable settings

Variable	Social				
Subvariable	Demographic Mix	Social Volatility	Education Level	Ethnic Diversity	Religious Diversity
Subvariable Settings	Balanced	Low	Limited	Single (Non-Competitive)	Single (Non-Competitive)
	Unbalanced, Gender	Moderate	Moderate	Multiple (Competitive, Single Predominant)	Multiple (Competitive, Single Predominant)
	Unbalanced, Age	High	High	Multiple (Competitive, None Predominant)	Multiple (Competitive, None Predominant)
	Unbalanced, Gender and Age				
Subvariable	Population Movement	Common Languages	Criminal Activity	Human Rights	
Subvariable Settings	Settled, Stable	Single	Limited	Women	
	Mixed	Multiple (One Preferred)	Moderate	Human Trafficking	
	Migrant	Multiple (None Preferred)	High	Child Warriors	
	IDPs			Torture	
	Refugees			Genocide	
				Slavery	

Table 3-21. Social: demographic mix

Definition: Descr bes the gender and military age balance of the population.		
Subvariable Setting	**Setting Definition**	**Considerations and Additional Notes**
Balanced	A population consisting of equal proportions of gender and military age.	
Unbalanced, Gender	A population consisting of an unequal proportion by gender (male, female) in relation to the overall group. The military age proportion of the population is not affected and remains the same as if it were in a balanced setting.	If an unstable society is desired in constructing an OE for training, this subvariable should be combined with other negative settings from other Social subvariables (see subvariable links below).
Unbalanced, Age	A population consisting of a greater proportion of the military age (male, female) in relation to the overall population. The gender proportion of the population is not affected and remains the same as if it were in a balanced setting.	(continued)

Table 3-21. Social: demographic mix (continued)

Subvariable Setting	Setting Definition	Considerations and Additional Notes
Unbalanced, Gender and Age	A population consisting of unequal proportions of gender (male, female) and military age in relation to the overall group.	
Subvariable Links: Political: Type of Government; Social: Social Volatility; Education Level, Criminal Activity, Human Rights.		

Table 3-22. Social: social volatility

Definition: Describes the amount of conflict between religious or ethnic groups present in a society and the amount of civil unrest present.		
Subvariable Setting	**Setting Definition**	**Considerations and Additional Notes**
Low	Low intergroup conflicts. Civil unrest is minimal. No significant refugee presence. High religious, ethnic, and political diversity.	1-2 preplanned or spontaneous riots or civil disorders based on religious or ethnic strife present within the scenario.
Moderate	Moderate intergroup conflicts. Civil unrest is sporadic. Minimal refugee presence. Some lack of religious, ethnic, and political diversity.	3-4 preplanned or spontaneous riots or civil disorders based on religious or ethnic strife present within the scenario.
High	High intergroup conflicts. Civil unrest is significant. Large refugee presence. Significant lack of religious, ethnic, and political diversity.	5-6 preplanned or spontaneous riots or civil disorders based on religious or ethnic strife present within the scenario.
Subvariable Links: Political: Government Effectiveness and Legitimacy; Social: Ethnic Diversity, Religious Diversity, Education Level.		

Table 3-23. Social: education level

Definition: Describes the education level of the population. (Helps determine the scripting requirements and may introduce specific scenario sub-themes into an OE.)		
Subvariable Setting	**Setting Definition**	**Considerations and Additional Notes**
Limited	Limited population literacy and education. Primitive education infrastructure and high unemployment.	Recommend 1/4 role-player population literate or educated for live training exercises. Limited education infrastructure and jobs (no more than 5%).
Moderate	Moderate population literacy and education. Some education infrastructure and moderate unemployment.	Recommend 1/2 role-player population literate or educated. Moderate amount of education infrastructure and jobs (no more than 10%).
High	High population literacy and education. Significant education infrastructure and low unemployment.	Recommend 3/4 role-player population literate or educated. High amount of education infrastructure and jobs (no more than 15%).
Subvariable Links: Political: Government Effectiveness and Legitimacy; Economic: Employment Status; Social: Social Volatility.		

Table 3-24. Social: ethnic diversity

Definition: Describes the number and specifies the interaction of various ethnic groups within a given population.		
Subvariable Setting	**Setting Definition**	**Considerations and Additional Notes**
Single Group, Non-Competitive	Self-explanatory.	

(continued)

Table 3-24. Social: ethnic diversity (continued)

Subvariable Setting	Setting Definition	Considerations and Additional Notes
Multiple Group, Competitive, Single Predominant	Up to three distinct ethnic groups distributed throughout a given area with one group clearly identifiable as the dominant population.	Role-player population with one group as the dominant population.
Multiple Group, Competitive, None Predominant	Three or more distinct ethnic groups distributed throughout a given area with no group designated as the dominant population.	Role-player population with no group designated as the dominant population.
Subvariable Links: Social: Religious Diversity, Social Volatility, Population Movement, Common Languages.		

Table 3-25. Social: religious diversity

Subvariable Setting	Setting Definition	Considerations and Additional Notes
Definition: Describes the number and specifies the interaction of various religious groups within a state or scenario population.		
Single Religion, Non-Competitive	Self-explanatory.	
Multiple Religions, Competitive, Single Predominant	Up to three distinct religious groups distributed within a given area with one group as the dominant population.	Role-player population with one group as the dominant population.
Multiple Religions, Competitive, None Predominant	Up to three distinct religious groups distributed within a given area with no group designated as the dominant population.	Role-player population with no group designated as the dominant population.
Subvariable Links: Social: Ethnic Diversity, Social Volatility, Population Movement, Common Languages.		

Table 3-26. Social: population movement

Subvariable Setting	Setting Definition	Considerations and Additional Notes
Definition: Describes the initial prevalence of migrant populations, internally displaced persons, and refugees within a country, region, or area. (This designation does not preclude the possibility of migrant populations as a result of the training unit's action or inaction.)		
Settled, Stable	Population is settled, organized, and does not move or displace except when confronted with occasions of extreme duress.	
Mixed	Part of population is settled and part moves frequently.	Population movement is based on the training unit's activities or pre-scripted as a scenario sub-event in response to training needs.
Migrant	Population frequently moves as a part of the normal state of affairs.	1-2 special mission elements' worth of role-players. Will cause the Political: Centers of Political Power subvariable to most likely be Tribal.
Internally Displaced Persons	A person who is involuntary moved inside the national boundaries of his or her country.	
Refugees	A person who, by reason of real or imagined danger, has left their home country or country of their nationality and is unwilling or unable to return.	
Subvariable Links: Economic: Employment Status; Economic Diversity; Social: Social Volatility, Common Languages.		

Table 3-27. Social: common languages

Definition: The preferred language(s) of a specific country or region or lack thereof.

Subvariable Setting	Setting Definition	Considerations and Additional Notes
Single Preferred and Predominant Language	Self-explanatory.	
Multiple Languages with One the Preferred Language	Country or region where several languages exist but one is recognized and used by the population as the preferred language.	For CTC replication, requires relatively high resources and support for an OE with multiple languages in terms of role-players and interpreters.
Multiple Languages with No Preferred or Predominant Language	Country or region where there is no preferred or predominant language. Frequently found in failed nation-states or states where the national language is not used except in specialized areas such as commerce.	Same as above.

Subvariable Links: Social: Demographic Mix, Ethnic Diversity, Population Movement.

Table 3-28. Social: criminal activity

Definition: Defines the level of criminal activity present in a society.

Subvariable Setting	Setting Definition	Considerations and Additional Notes
Limited	Limited criminal activity.	For CTC replication, 1-2 activities present from criminal activity. Limited to up to 30% of the total urban landscape.
Moderate	Moderate criminal activity present.	For CTC replication, 1-3 activities present from criminal activity. Limited to up to 50% of the total urban landscape. Presence of at least one criminal gang distributed throughout the scenario environment.
High	High criminal activity present.	For CTC replication, 3-4 activities present from criminal activity. Two or more rival criminal gangs or organizations present and active in the scenario (manifested by competition, gang or mob warfare). Limited to presence in 75% of the total urban landscape.

Subvariable Links: Political: Type of Government; Military: Non-State Paramilitary Forces; Economic: Illegal Economic Activity.

Table 3-29. Social: human rights

Definition: *Human rights* refer to the basic rights and freedoms to which all humans are entitled. Examples of rights and freedoms that have come to be commonly thought of as human rights include: civil and political rights, such as the right to life and liberty, freedom of expression, and equality before the law; and economic and social rights, including the right to participate in culture, the right to food, the right to work, and the right to education.

The most widely recognized international documentation of human rights is the 1948 UN Universal Declaration of Human Rights (UDHR), which has been ratified by the majority of the world's nations. However, many nations still struggle or refuse to implement all of the provisions of this declaration. Understanding whether and to what extent each country or region is complying with internationally recognized human rights is critical to the success of military operations. Below are some of the more blatant areas of violation within human rights. These are areas the U.S. military has faced in the recent past that may be important to understand in a future AO.

Subvariable Setting	Setting Definition	Considerations and Additional Notes
Women	Issues relating to the political, economic, civil, social, and educational rights of women.	Examples of issues related to these areas are voting rights, employment discrimination, sexual discrimination, honor killings, forced and early marriages, reproductive rights, health care, and educational discrimination.

(continued)

Table 3-29. Social: human rights (continued)

Subvariable Setting	Setting Definition	Considerations and Additional Notes
Human Trafficking	Human trafficking is the commerce and trade in the movement or migration of people, legal and illegal, including legitimate labor activities as well as forced labor. The term is used in a more narrow sense by advocacy groups to mean the recruitment, transportation, harboring, or receipt of people for the purposes of slavery, prostitution, forced labor (including bonded labor or debt bondage), and servitude.	Human trafficking is the fastest growing criminal industry in the world, with the total annual revenue for trafficking in persons estimated to be between $5 billion and $9 billion. (Fact Sheet 1, Economic Roots of Trafficking in the UNECE Region, Geneva, 15 Dec 04).
Child Warriors	Child warriors are the result of forced or compulsory recruitment of anyone under the age of 18 for use in armed conflict. This can include children taking direct part in hostilities or used in support roles such as porters, spies, messengers, or lookouts.	In over 20 countries around the world, children are direct participants in war. Denied a childhood and often subjected to horrific violence, an estimated 200,000 to 300,000 children are serving as soldiers for both rebel groups and government forces in current armed conflicts.
Torture	Torture, according to the UN Convention Against Torture, is: "any act by which severe pain and suffering, whether physical or mental, is intentionally inflicted on a person for such purposes as obtaining from him, or a third person, information or a confession, punishing him for an act he or a third person has committed or is suspected of having committed, or intimidating or coercing him or a third person, or for any reason based on discrimination of any kind, when such pain or suffering is inflicted by or at the instigation of or with the consent or acquiescence of a public official or other person acting in an official capacity. It does not include pain or suffering arising only from, inherent in, or incidental to, lawful sanctions."	Torture is widely considered to be a violation of human rights, and is declared to be unacceptable by Article 5 of the UN Universal Declaration of Human Rights. Signatories of the Third Geneva Convention and Fourth Geneva Convention officially agree not to torture prisoners in armed conflicts. Torture is also prohibited by the UN Convention Against Torture, which has been ratified by 145 states. However, Amnesty International estimates that at least 81 world governments currently practice torture, some openly.
Genocide	The 1948 UN Convention on the Prevention and Punishment of the Crime of Genocide (CPPCG). Article 2, defines genocide as: "any of the following acts committed with intent to destroy, in whole or in part, a national, ethnical, racial, or religious group, as such: killing members of the group; causing serious bodily or mental harm to members of the group; deliberately inflicting on the group conditions of life, calculated to bring about its physical destruction in whole or in part; imposing measures intended to prevent births within the group; [and] forcibly transferring children of the group to another group."	To commit genocide, the perpetrators need a strong, centralized authority and bureaucratic organization as well as pathological individuals and criminals. Also required is a campaign of vilification and dehumanization of the victims by the perpetrators, who are usually new states or new regimes attempting to impose conformity to a new ideology and its model of society. Examples of recent acts of genocide are Rwanda, Former Yugoslavia, and Sudan.
Slavery	Slavery is a form of forced labor in which people are considered to be, or treated as, the property of others. Slaves are held against their will from the time of their capture, purchase, or birth, and are deprived of the right to leave, to refuse to work, or to receive compensation (such as wages).	Evidence of slavery predates written records, and has existed to varying extents, forms and periods in almost all cultures and continents. In some societies, slavery existed as a legal institution or socio-economic system, but today it is formally outlawed in nearly all countries. Nevertheless, the practice continues in various forms around the world. Freedom from slavery is an internationally recognized human right. Article 4 of the UDHR states: "No one shall be held in slavery or servitude; slavery and the slave trade shall be prohibited in all their forms."

Subvariable Links: Political: Type of Government; Military: Non-State Paramilitary Forces; Economic: Illegal Economic Activity.

INFORMATION VARIABLE

3-13. The Information variable describes the nature, scope, characteristics, and effects of individuals, organizations, and systems that collect, process, disseminate, or act on information. Information involves the access, use, manipulation, distribution, and reliance on information technology systems, both civilian and military, by an entity (state or non-state). Understanding whatever communication infrastructure exists in an OE is important because it ultimately controls the flow of information to the population and military and/or paramilitary forces, as well as influencing local and international audiences. Communication availability can act as a leveling function with regard to mitigating military technical advantages to a surprising extent. Military units must understand and engage in the information environment in order to achieve their objectives. The specific information subvariables and their settings represent replicable conditions that may be present within an OE and are depicted in table 3-30. Their associated definitions, considerations, additional notes, and external links are listed separately in tables 3-31 through 3-34.

Table 3-30. Information variable and subvariable settings

Variable	Information			
Subvariable	Public Communications Media	Information Warfare	Intelligence	Information Management
Subvariable Settings	Internet	Electronic Warfare	Open-Source Intelligence	Rudimentary
	Television	Computer Warfare	Human Intelligence	Basic
	Radio	Information Attack	Signals Intelligence	Medium
	Print Media	Deception	Imagery Intelligence	Advanced
	Telephone	Physical Destruction		
	Postal and Courier Service	Protection and Security Measures		
	Word of Mouth	Perception Management		

Table 3-31. Information: public communications media

Definition: Descr bes the type of information or media sources that may be available to the public in an OE.		
(The individual media as sub-subvariables can have settings reflecting the level of availability: None = nonexistent; Limited = available in large cities only; Moderate = available in cities and some towns; Widespread = available down to town level.)		
Subvariable Setting	**Setting Definition**	**Considerations and Additional Notes**
Internet	Self-explanatory.	Interruptible, 4-5 building intranet access per town, capable of replicating an Internet capable of hosting at least 6 dynamic pages or sites consisting of the following site types: 2 weblogs, 2 Internet chat rooms, and 2 news websites.
Television	Self-explanatory.	A single channel, cable broadcast capability with a connected studio production site (located in exercise area), associated personnel, and sufficient programming to broadcast 10 hours per day.

(continued)

Table 3-31. Information: public communications media (continued)

Subvariable Setting	Setting Definition	Considerations and Additional Notes
Radio	Self-explanatory.	An AM or FM radio broadcast station, with associated personnel, and the ability to broadcast programming for 10 hours per day for the duration of an exercise. Broadcast and studio facilities would ideally be located in the exercise area to enhance play.
Print Media	Self-explanatory.	Media personnel (role-players) and associated equipment required to create and locally produce a single-page newspaper or flyer. Minimum of one production element present per 2 towns.
Telephone	Self-explanatory.	Landline and/or mobile telephone service.
Postal and Courier Service	Self-explanatory.	Postal or courier personnel (role-players) and associated transportation means.
Word of Mouth	Self-explanatory.	Scripted instructions to role-players to report specific information, relay certain data, or to spontaneously report on specific activities.
Subvariable Links: Economic: Banking and Finance; Social: Social Volatility, Ethnic Diversity, Criminal Activity, Common Languages; Information: Information Management; Infrastructure: Utility Level, Utilities Present, Transportation Architecture.			

Table 3-32. Information: information warfare

Definition: *Information warfare* (INFOWAR) is the specifically planned and integrated actions taken to achieve an information advantage at critical points and times. (FM 7-100.1) INFOWAR consists of seven elements: electronic warfare (EW), computer warfare, information attack, deception, physical destruction, protection and security measures, and perception management. These elements do not exist in isolation from one another and are not mutually exclusive. (FM 7-100.1)

(INFOWAR elements as sub-subvariables can have settings on a scale of 1 to 5: 1 = Very Limited; 2 = Limited; 3 = Moderate; 4 = Good; 5 = Superior.)

Subvariable Setting	Setting Definition	Considerations and Additional Notes
Electronic Warfare	Consists of countermeasures conducted to control or deny other actors' use of the electromagnetic spectrum, while ensuring one's own use of it. EW capabilities allow an actor to exploit, deceive, degrade, disrupt, damage, or destroy sensors, processors, and C2 nodes. (FM 7-100.1)	At a minimum, the goal of EW is to control the use of the electromagnetic spectrum at critical locations and times or to attack a specific system. To accomplish these EW goals and objectives, actors can employ both lethal and nonlethal measures. *Lethal EW* activities include the physical destruction of high-priority targets supporting another actor's decisionmaking process—such as reconnaissance sensors, command posts, and communications systems. They also include activities such as lethal air defense suppression measures. If available, precision munitions can degrade or eliminate high-technology C2 assets and associated links. *Nonlethal EW* means range from signals reconnaissance and electronic jamming to the deployment of protective countermeasures and deception jammers. Sophisticated camouflage, deception, decoy, or mockup systems can degrade the effects of enemy reconnaissance, intelligence, surveillance, and target acquisition (RISTA) systems. Also, an actor can employ low-cost GPS jammers to disrupt another actor's precision munitions targeting, sensor-to-shooter links, and navigation. (FM 7-100.1)

(continued)

Table 3-32. Information: information warfare (continued)

Subvariable Setting	Setting Definition	Considerations and Additional Notes
Computer Warfare	Consists of attacks that focus specifically on computer systems, networks, and/or nodes. This includes a wide variety of activities, ranging from unauthorized access (hacking) of information systems for intelligence-collection purposes, to the insertion of malicious software (viruses, worms, logic bombs, or Trojan horses) and deceptive information entry into computer systems. Such attacks concentrate on the denial of service and disruption or manipulation of the integrity of the information infrastructure. (FM 7-100.1)	Actors may attempt to accomplish these activities through the use of agents or third-party individuals with direct access to another actor's information systems. They can also continually access and attack systems at great distances via communications links such as the Internet or various wireless devices. (FM 7-100.1)
Information Attack	An *information attack* (IA) focuses on the intentional disruption or distortion of information in a manner that supports a comprehensive INFOWAR campaign. Unlike computer warfare attacks that target the information systems, IAs target the information itself. (FM 7-100.1)	An IA may target an information system for sabotage (electronically or physically) or manipulate and exploit information. This may involve altering data, stealing data, or forcing a system to perform a function for which it was not intended. (FM 7-100.1)
Deception	Deception activities include measures designed to mislead adversaries by manipulation, distortion, or falsification of information. The aim of deception is to influence opponents' situational understanding and lead them to act in a manner that is prejudicial to their own interests or favors the actor employing the deception. (FM 7-100.1)	Deception measures are a part of every military operation, and are also used to achieve political and economic goals. The international media may be a target for deceptive information at the operational level, being fed false stories and video that portrays tactical-level actions with the goal of influencing operational or even strategic decisions. (FM 7-100.1)

Forms of deception that support IW range from physical decoys and electronic devices, to operational activities, to casualty "photo ops" staged for unsuspecting media personnel. Successful deception activities depend on the identification and exploitation of enemy information systems and networks, as well as other "conduits" for introducing deceptive information. (FM 7-100.1) |
| Physical Destruction | Physical destruction, as an element of INFOWAR, involves measures to destroy critical components of the enemy's information infrastructure. (FM 7-100.1) | The OPFOR integrates all types of conventional and precision weapon systems to conduct the destructive fires, to include fixed- and rotary-wing aviation, cannon artillery, multiple rocket launchers, and surface-to-surface missiles. It can also utilize other means of destruction, such as explosives delivered by special-purpose forces (SPF), insurgents, terrorists, or even co-opted civilians. Physical destruction activities can be integrated with jamming to maximize their effects. (FM 7-100.1) |
| Protection and Security Measures | The purpose of protection and security measures in INFOWAR is to protect one's own information infrastructure, maintain one's own capabilities for effective C2, and deny protected information to other actors. (FM 7-100.1) | Protection and security measures conducted as part of INFOWAR include—
• Information collection, processing, and utilization.
• Reconnaissance and counterreconnaissance.
• Information and operations security.
• Camouflage, concealment, cover, and deception.
• Force protection.
• Secure use of information-collection and –processing systems.
An actor's capability against its main opponent can come from a high-tech asset or a low-tech approach. (FM 7-100.1) |

(continued)

Table 3-32. Information: information warfare (continued)

Subvariable Setting	Setting Definition	Considerations and Additional Notes
Perception Management	Perception management involves measures aimed at creating a perception of truth that furthers an actor's objective. It integrates several widely differing activities that use a combination of true, false, misleading, or manipulated information. (FM 7-100.1)	Enemy or foreign audiences, as well as the local population, may be targets of perception management. Perception management can include misinformation, media manipulation, and psychological warfare. (FM 7-100.1) *Psychological warfare* (PSYWAR) is the capability and activities designed to influence selected friendly, neutral, and/or hostile target audiences' attitudes and behaviors in support of the actor. PSYWAR can target either specific decisionmaking systems or the entire information system of the target audience, while influencing key communicators and decisionmakers. Such attacks target an enemy's perceived centers of gravity. For example, prolonging an operation and using all forms of media to show the devastation of conflict can sway public opinion against the effort. (FM 7-100.1) Many actors skillfully employ media and other neutral actors, such as NGOs, to influence further public and private perceptions. Actors can exploit the international media's willingness to report information without independent and timely confirmation. Individuals such as agents of influence, sympathizers, and antiwar protesters are also employed advantageously to influence the enemy's media, politicians, and citizenry. (FM 7-100.1)
Subvariable Links: Military: Military Functions; Information: Information Management; Infrastructure: Utility Level, Utilities Present.		

Table 3-33. Information: intelligence

Definition: The product resulting from the collection, processing, integration, evaluation, analysis, and interpretation of available information concerning foreign nations, hostile or potentially hostile forces or elements, or areas of actual or potential operations. The term is also applied to the activity which results in the product and to the organizations engaged in such activity. (JP 2-0)

Subvariable Setting	Setting Definition	Considerations and Additional Notes
Open-Source Intelligence (OSINT)	Information of potential intelligence value that is available to the general public. (JP 2-0) OSINT is derived from the systematic collection, processing, and analysis of publicly available, relevant information in response to intelligence requirements. (FM 2-0)	OSINT is produced from publicly available information that is collected, exploited, and disseminated in a timely manner to an appropriate audience for the purpose of addressing a specific intelligence requirement. (National Defense Authorization Act for Fiscal Year 2006)
Human Intelligence (HUMINT)	A category of intelligence derived from information collected and provided by human sources. (JP 2-0) HUMINT is the collection or foreign information—by a trained HUMINT collector—from people and multimedia to identify elements, intentions, composition, strength, dispositions, tactics, equipment, personnel, and capabilities. It uses human sources as a tool and a variety of collection methods, both passively and actively, to collect information. (FM 2-0)	Special-purpose forces (SPF) are a major source of human intelligence (HUMINT). (FM 7-100.1)

(continued)

Table 3-33. Information: intelligence (continued)

Subvariable Setting	Setting Definition	Considerations and Additional Notes
Signals Intelligence (SIGINT)	1. A category of intelligence comprising either individually or in combination all communications intelligence, electronic intelligence, and foreign instrumentation signals intelligence, however transmitted. 2. Intelligence derived from communications, electronic, and foreign instrumentation signals. (JP 1-02) SIGINT is intelligence produced by exploiting foreign communication systems and noncommunications emitters. (JP 2-0) The SIGINT discipline is comprised of communications intelligence (COMINT), electronic intelligence (ELINT), and foreign instrumentation signals intelligence (FISINT). (FM 2-0)	In OPFOR terminology, *signals reconnaissance* is an integral part of information warfare. The overall scope of signals reconnaissance includes the interception, analysis, and exploitation of electromagnetic (radio and radar) emissions, coupled with measures to disrupt or destroy the enemy's radio and radar assets. (FM 7-100.1)
Imagery Intelligence (IMINT)	The technical, geographic, and intelligence information derived through the interpretation or analysis of imagery and collateral materials. (JP 2-03)	IMINT is intelligence derived from the exploitation of imagery collected by visual photography, infrared, lasers, multi-spectral sensors, and radar. These sensors produce images of objects optically, electronically, or digitally on film, electronic display devices, or other media. (FM 2-0)
Subvariable Links: Military: Military Functions; Social: Education Level; Information: Information Warfare, Information Management.		

Table 3-34. Information: information management

Definition: *Information Management* is the science of using procedures and information systems to collect, process, store, display, disseminate, and protect knowledge products, data, and information. (FM 3-0). It employs both staff management and automatic processes to focus a vast array of information and make relevant information available to the right person at the right time. Effective information management—synchronized with reconnaissance, intelligence, surveillance, and target acquisition (RISTA) operations—enables commanders to gain and maintain information superiority. The level of Information management is defined by management, systems, and security. The three are intertwined and are therefore addressed as a composite capability in this subvariable.

Information Systems: The equipment and facilities that collect, process, store, display and disseminate information. This includes computers—hardware and software—and communications, as well as policies and procedures for their use. (FM 3-0) Information systems and information management appear similar because they are intertwined. The sophistication of the information systems largely determines the capability of military command and control (C2) and civil interconnectivity.

Information Security: The protection of information and information systems against unauthorized access or modification of information, whether in storage, processing, or transit, and against denial of services to authorized users. (JP 3-13) Information security includes those measures necessary to detect, document, and counter such threats. Information security is composed of computer security and communications security.

Subvariable Setting	Setting Definition	Considerations and Additional Notes
Rudimentary	Individuals or small groups supported by state-sponsored institutions (military or civilian) and non-state international groups. **Military** uses computers, analog, Internet, cell phones, radios, satellite phones, etc. Limited-to-no military automated information management systems. **Commercial**, business, and finance stand-alone systems. Communications systems separate but basic. 0 to 24% encrypted (secure).	*Relevant information* is all information of importance to commanders and staffs in the exercise of command and control. (FM 3-0) *Information superiority* is the operational advantage derived from the ability to collect, process, and disseminate an uninterrupted flow of information while exploiting or denying an adversary's ability to do the same (JP 3-13).

(continued)

Table 3-34. Information: information management (continued)

Subvariable Setting	Setting Definition	Considerations and Additional Notes
Basic	Integrated digital information management systems. **Military:** digitized: computerized reports, direct GPS and encryption (selected), direct sensor-to-shooter links, laser range-finders, Internet, broadcast tactical warning systems. **Commercial**, business, communications and finance systems linked locally but not integrated. 25% to 50% encrypted (secure).	Allows commanders to take advantage of opportunities, while denying adversary commanders the information needed to make timely and accurate decisions or leading them to make decisions favorable to friendly forces.
Medium	Windows of information domination. **Military:** integrated battlefield management systems, integrated C2, navigation, fire control, RISTA, image, maps, video, encrypted to battalion level, with or without SATCOM, GPS to squad level. Some **commercial**, business, communications and finance systems integrated locally, others linked. Some linked internationally. 51% to 75% encrypted (secure).	
Advanced	Advanced (state-of-the-art) information systems. Maintains information superiority. Creates conditions that allow commanders to shape the OE and enhance the effects of all elements of combat power. **Military:** U.S. Joint Tactical Information Distribution System (JTIDS) and/or Blue (& Red) Force Tracker or foreign equivalent. Technological advancements in automated information systems and communications allow commanders to see the battlefield as actions unfold, near real-time, and to rapidly pass information across their AOs. **Commercial**, business, communications, and finance systems integrated locally and internationally. 76% to 90% encrypted (secure).	

Subvariable Links: Military: Military Functions; Social: Education Level; Information: Information Warfare; Infrastructure: Utility Level.

INFRASTRUCTURE VARIABLE

3-14. The Infrastructure variable is composed of the basic facilities, services, and installations needed for the functioning of a community or society. The degradation or destruction of infrastructure will impact the entire OE, especially the Political, Military, Economic, Social, and Information variables. This variable also reflects the infrastructure sophistication of an OE. The specific infrastructure subvariables and their settings represent replicable conditions that may be present within an OE and are depicted in table 3-35. Their associated definitions, considerations, additional notes, and external links are listed separately in tables 3-36 through 3-41.

Table 3-35. Infrastructure variable and subvariable settings

Variable	Infrastructure					
Subvariable	Construc-tion Pattern	Urban Zones	Urbanized Building Density	Utilities Present	Utility Level	Transportation Architecture
Subvariable Settings	Dense, Random	City Core	Low	Power	Non-Existent	Primitive
	Close Orderly Block	Core Periphery	Medium	Water	Degraded	Moderate
	Strip Area	High-Rise Residential	High	Sewage	Developed	Complex
	Shantytown	Low-Rise Residential		Services and Transportation		
		Commercial Area				
		Industrial Area				
		Military Area				

Table 3-36. Infrastructure: construction pattern

Definition: The physical layout of buildings and streets in an urban area (village, town, or city).		
Subvariable Setting	**Setting Definition**	**Considerations and Additional Notes**
Dense, Random Construction	Urban area consisting of closely packed build-ings with little set-back from narrow winding streets that often radiate in an irregular manner from a single area, such as a religious building, dock area, or government center.	This construction pattern is typical in old walled towns and cities and old port towns and cities. Frequently found in city core and core periphery zones. May also be found in towns and villages.
Close Orderly Block Construction	Urban area consisting of residential and commercial type buildings forming distinct rec-tangular blocks. Buildings frequently share a continuous front along the street for as much as a city block, and inner-block courtyards are common. Streets are generally wider and form rectangular patterns.	This construction pattern is often typical of a designed or planned urban area. Frequently found in city core and core periphery zones.

(continued)

Table 3-36. Infrastructure: construction pattern (continued)

Subvariable Setting	Setting Definition	Considerations and Additional Notes
Strip Area	A strip area is a small urban area predominately built along a transportation route, such as a road or river. Usually assumes a long, thin, linear pattern.	The strip area may stand alone or be linked between nearby larger urban areas. If visibility is good and enough effective fields of fire are available, a unit acting as a security force need occupy only a few strong positions spread out within the strip. This will deceive the enemy, when engaged at long ranges, into thinking the strip is an extensive defensive line. Strip areas often afford covered avenues of withdrawal to the flanks once the attacking force is deployed and before the security force becomes decisively engaged.
Shantytown	Random arrangement of poorly constructed structures made of any scrap material available, irregularly laid out, and connected by walking paths that may not accommodate vehicular traffic.	Shantytowns are typically areas composed of low income or unemployed elements of the population who live in poorly constructed buildings or older buildings in various states of decay. Most towns and villages in third world countries have shantytowns that often can be found in multiple zones throughout the area. Structures within shantytowns are constructed from readily available materials, such as cardboard, tin, adobe, or concrete block. These less structurally sound buildings have no common floor pattern and are more likely to have only one room. Random arrangement of structures, absence of formal street naming, and often the lack of easily identifiable buildings and terrain create challenges. The temporary nature of the structures can mean that mobility can be either more or less restricted than other sections of an urban area. Mobility becomes more restrictive as the narrow paths often do not accommodate vehicles. Weak structures afford little protection and increase the risk of fratricide, civilian casualties, and large, rapidly spreading fires.

Subvariable Links: Military: Military Forces; Economics: Economic Diversity; Infrastructure: Urban Zones, Urbanized Building Density.

Table 3-37. Infrastructure: urban zones

Definition: Distinct areas or zones within a city that is geographically identifiable. These zones are normally categorized by the predominate activity within their boundaries.

Subvariable Setting	Setting Definition	Considerations and Additional Notes
City Core	The city core is the heart of the urban area—the downtown or central business district. It is relatively small and compact but contains a large percentage of the urban area's shops, offices, and public institutions. It normally contains the highest density of multistory buildings and subterranean areas. Older city cores have narrow streets (7 to 15 m wide), while newer, planned developments have wider streets (at least 15 to 25 m wide). In most cities, the core has undergone more recent development than the core periphery. As a result, the two regions are often quite different. Typical city cores are made up of buildings that vary greatly in height.	Buildings 15-20 stories and higher (possibly up to 50 stories above ground and 4 stories below ground). Older city cores have few open areas and buildings are closer to streets, but modern urban planning allows for more open spaces. Large workforce; few residents. Dense random and close orderly block are two common construction patterns that can be found within the city core.

(continued)

Table 3-37. Infrastructure: urban zones (continued)

Subvariable Setting	Setting Definition	Considerations and Additional Notes
Core Periphery	The core periphery is located at the outer edges of the city core. The core periphery consists of streets 12 to 20 m wide with continuous fronts of brick or concrete buildings. The building heights are fairly uniform—2 or 3 stories in small towns, five to ten stories in large cities.	Buildings 2-10 stories. Few open areas (but more than in city core). Large workforce; average residents. Dense random and close orderly block are two common construction patterns that can be found within core periphery zones.
High-Rise Residential Area	Typical of modern construction in larger cities and towns, this area consists of multistoried apartments. Wide streets are laid out in rectangular patterns. Rarely are there unbroken rows of houses facing the street in this type area.	Buildings 15-20 stories and higher. Limited open areas (such as parking lots, recreation areas, parks, and individual one-story buildings). Average workforce; average residents. These areas are often contiguous to industrial or transportation areas or interspersed with close orderly block areas.
Low-Rise Residential Area	Dispersed row houses or single-family dwellings with yards, gardens, trees, and fences. Street patterns are normally rectangular or curving. However, buildings are normally set back from the road.	Buildings 1-3 stories. Many open areas. Small workforce; many residents. Residential zones are typically subdivided by income or culturally important factors, such as ethnicity or religion. This type area is normally contiguous to close orderly block areas in Europe. In some areas of the world, residential areas may be located in high walled compounds with houses built right up to the edge of the street.
Commercial Area	Rows of stores, shops, and restaurants built along both sides of major streets that run through and between urban areas. Streets are usually 25 m wide or more. The buildings uniformly stand 2 to 3 stories tall (about one story taller than the dwellings on the streets behind them).	Buildings 2-3 stories. Subcategories are commercial ribbon areas built along major streets in an urban area or strip areas built along the roads that connect one urban area to another.
Industrial Area	Industrial areas are generally located on or along major rail and highway routes in urban complexes. Older complexes may be located within dense, random construction or close orderly block areas. New construction normally consists of low, flat-roofed factory and warehouse buildings (1 to 3 stories) in dispersed, irregular patterns with large parking areas and work yards.	Buildings 1-5 stories. Many open areas. Large workforce; few residents. Industrial areas often develop on the outskirts of urban areas, where commercial transportation is easiest (along airfields and major sea, river, rail, and highway routes). High-rise areas providing worker housing are normally located adjacent to these areas throughout Asia. Identification of transportation facilities within these areas is critical because these facilities, especially rail facilities, pose significant obstacles to military movement. Toxic industrial chemicals and other hazardous materials may be transported or stored throughout the industrial area.
Military Area (Permanent or Fixed Fortifications)	These include any of several different types and may be actual fortifications. These permanent fortifications can be made of earth, wood, rock, brick, concrete, steel-reinforced concrete, or any combination of the above. Some of the latest variants are built underground and employ heavy tank or warship armor, major caliber and other weapons, internal communications, service facilities, and CBRN overpressure systems.	Defense oriented; planned positions. Usually regular armed forces. May be found in or near urban areas (which may have grown up around the military installation that provided protection for inhabitants).

Subvariable Links: Military: Military Forces; Economics: Economic Diversity; Social: Volatility; Infrastructure: Construction Pattern.

Table 3-38. Infrastructure: urbanized building density

Definition: Descrbes the average building density within a town.		
Subvariable Setting	Setting Definition	Considerations and Additional Notes
Low	Less than 15 buildings per town with no 2-story structures. Single economic industry structures present in each town.	
Medium	15 to 25 buildings per town with at least 3 multi-story structures. One government center (5-building cluster) and site of significance (3-building cluster) per province. Two economic industry structures present per town.	
High	25 or more buildings per town with at least 5 multi-story structures clustered together or separated by a one-story building or open area. One government center (5-building cluster) and one site of significance (a 3-building cluster) per district. Three economic industry structures and constructions present in the OE.	
Subvariable Links: Military: Military Forces; Infrastructure: All; Physical Environment: Terrain Complexity, Obstacles.		

Table 3-39. Infrastructure: utilities present

Definition: Descrbes the average building density within a town.		
Subvariable Setting	Setting Definition	Considerations and Additional Notes
Low	Less than 15 buildings per town with no 2-story structures. Single economic industry structures present in each town.	
Medium	15 to 25 buildings per town with at least 3 multi-story structures. One government center (5-building cluster) and site of significance (3-building cluster) per province. Two economic industry structures present per town.	
High	25 or more buildings per town with at least 5 multi-story structures clustered together or separated by a one-story building or open area. One government center (5-building cluster) and one site of significance (a 3-building cluster) per district. Three economic industry structures and constructions present in the OE.	
Subvariable Links: Military: Military Forces; Infrastructure: All; Physical Environment: Terrain Complexity, Obstacles.		

Table 3-40. Infrastructure: utility level

Definition: Describes the approximate percentage of utilities available to a town. Each utility present in the OE has its own respective service level.		
Subvariable Setting	Setting Definition	Considerations and Additional Notes
Non-Existent	25% present and operational.	25% of all distribution nodes or required infra-structure and role-player elements/material are present or operational, with physical distribution and services present to at least 1/4 of the structures in each "switched on" area.

(continued)

Table 3-40. Infrastructure: utility level (continued)

Subvariable Setting	Setting Definition	Considerations and Additional Notes
Degraded	50% present and operational.	50% of all distribution nodes or required infrastructure and role-player elements/material are present or operational, with physical distribution and services present to at least 1/3 of the structures in each "switched on" area.
Developed	75% present and operational.	75% of all distribution nodes or required infrastructure and role-player elements/material are present or operational, with physical distribution and services present to at least half of the structures in each "switched on" area.
Subvariable Links: Political: Government Effectiveness; Economic: Economic Diversity; Social: Social Volatility; Infrastructure: All.		

Table 3-41. Infrastructure: transportation architecture

Definition: Details the existing public road and transportation network present in an OE. Describes the type of roads present and the coverage of the road network to any built-up areas. Includes airports, ports, rail, and surface road networks.		
Subvariable Setting	**Setting Definition**	**Considerations and Additional Notes**
Primitive	Single track or improved two-lane hard-surface road networks, extending to all built-up areas. Single-line railway, no functioning airports, limited or no riverine transportation networks.	Definitions also set the material and scenario scripting requirements associated with each replicated service.
Moderate	Improved multi-lane hard-surface road networks, extending to all built-up areas with secondary, two-lane hard-surface roads paralleling primary roads. Two to three 2-line railways, connecting at least 50% of the OE infrastructure. One functioning airport and, if present, moderate riverine transportation networks.	
Complex	Multi-lane hard-surface highway networks, extending to all built-up areas with secondary, multi-lane hard-surface roads paralleling primary roads. Three to four 2-line railways, connecting at least 75% of the OE infrastructure. Two to three large, functioning airports (jet capable) and, if present, extensive riverine transportation networks.	
Subvariable Links: Political: Government Effectiveness; Military: Military Forces; Economic: Economic Diversity; Infrastructure: All.		

PHYSICAL ENVIRONMENT VARIABLE

3-15. The Physical Environment variable includes the geography and man-made structures as well as the climate and weather in the AO. Depending on the type of exercise, these conditions may be real, notional, or a combination. The span of subvariables defining the Physical Environment includes "terrain," "natural hazards," "climate," and "weather," depicted in table 3-42. The detail and complexity of the "terrain" and "weather" subvariables necessitate breaking down some of their components beyond the subvariable level. This lower level classification is called *sub-subvariable*. Some of the components of "terrain" are actually sub-subvariables, and all components of the "weather" subvariable require this additional breakdown. (See table 3-43 on page 3-32.)

Table 3-42. Physical Environment variable and subvariable settings

Variable	Physical Environment			
Subvariable	Terrain	Natural Hazards	Climate	Weather
Subvariable Settings	Observation and Fields of Fire	Volcanoes	Tropical	Precipitation
	Avenues of Approach	Drought	Arid	High Temperature—Heat Index
	Key Terrain	Monsoon	Mediterranean	Low Temperature—Wind Chill Index
	Obstacles	Earthquake	Oceanic	Wind
	Cover and Concealment	Flooding	Continental	Visibility
Sub-Subvariable	Landforms	Avalanche	Subarctic	Cloud Cover
	Vegetation	Cyclone		Relative Humidity
	Terrain Complexity	Other (Diseases)		See table 3-43 for an overview of sub-subvariable settings.
	Mobility Classification			

Table 3-43. Physical Environment variable, subvariables and sub-subvariable settings

Variable	Physical Environment						
Subvariable	Terrain						
Sub-Subvariable	Landforms	Vegetation	Terrain Complexity	Mobility Classification			
Sub-Subvariable Settings	Sloped	Desert/Scrub	Urban Area-Plus Other	Unrestricted Terrain			
	Coastal	Grassland	Urban Area Alone	Restricted Terrain			
	Fluvial	Woodland	Two or More Types of Restrictive Terrain	Severely Restricted Terrain			
	Erosion	Mixed	Single Type of Restrictive Terrain				
	Mountain/Glacial		Unrestricted				
	Mixed						
Subvariable	Weather						
Sub-Subvariable	Precipitation	High Temperature—Heat Index	Low Temperature—Wind Chill Index	Wind	Visibility	Cloud Cover	Relative Humidity
Sub-Subvariables Settings	Very Light	75-85°F	1 mph at 50°F to 40 mph at 20°F	Calm	Beginning Morning Nautical Twilight	Clear	WBGT Index reaches 78°F
	Light	85-105°F	1 mph at -30°F to 40 mph at -10°F	Moderate Breeze	Beginning Morning Civil Twilight	Scattered	WBGT Index reaches 85°F
	Moderate	95-130°F	10 mph at -50°F to 40 mph at -60°F	Strong Breeze	End of Evening Civil Twilight	Broken	WBGT Index reaches 88°F
	Heavy	95-130°F		Moderate Gale	End of Evening Nautical Twilight	Overcast	WBGT Index reaches 90°F
		Over 130°F		Strong Gale			
				Storm			

3-16. The next level of discussion is to graphically portray the associated definitions of each Physical Environment subvariable and sub-subvariable as well as their settings, setting definitions, considerations and additional notes and external links with other subvariables. (See tables 3-44 through 3-58.) This format is designed to give the exercise planner the necessary details needed for constructing the desired OE. The order of discussion will be "terrain," "natural hazards," "climate," and "weather."

TERRAIN

3-17. Definitions of "terrain" and the associated subvariable setting definitions are listed in table 3-44. In this case, the subvariable settings are actually a menu of certain aspects of terrain that need to be taken into consideration. The last four subvariable settings are actually sub-subvariables that have their own definitions and settings (see tables 3-45 through 3-48). Limitations inherent with specific types of terrain are enforced by observer-controllers in live exercises or by computer-enforced rules in simulated exercises.

Table 3-44. Physical environment: terrain

Definition: *Terrain* is a portion of the earth's surface that includes natural and manmade features (TC 2-33.4).		
Subvariable Setting	**Setting or Sub-Subvariable Definition**	**Considerations and Additional Notes**
Observation and Fields of Fire	*Observation* is the condition of weather and terrain that permits a force to see personnel, systems, and key aspects of the environment (FM 2-01.3). *Field of fire* is the area which a weapon or a group of weapons may cover effectively with fire from a given position. (JP 1-02 and FM 1-02)	The type of units (friendly and enemy) which are on the ground, how they look from each other's perspective on the battlefield, and lines of sight (LOS) from their positions to the target (TC 2-33.4). Intervisibility is the condition of being able to see one point from the other. (FM 2-01.3)
Avenues of Approach	An *avenue of approach* (AA) is an air or ground route of an attacking force of a given size leading to its objective or to key terrain in its path. (JP 1-02)	Mobility corridors (MCs) are subsets of AAs. To evaluate and develop AAs, the results developed during obstacle evaluation are used to identify and categorize MCs and to group MCs into AAs. (FM 2-01.3). [See Physical Environment: Terrain: Mobility Classification.] *Mobility corridors* are areas where a force will be canalized due to terrain restrictions; they allow military forces to capitalize on the principles of mass and speed and are therefore relatively free of obstacles. (JP 2-01.3)
Key Terrain	*Key terrain* is any locality or area whose seizure, retention, or control affords a marked advantage to either combatant. (JP 2-01.3, FM 2-01.3, and TC 2-33.4)	Any terrain that increases a unit's ability to apply combat power, or decreases the opponent's ability to apply theirs, is considered key terrain. (TC 2-33.4)
Obstacles	An *obstacle* is any obstruction designed or employed to disrupt, fix, turn, or block the movement of an opposing force [enemy], and to impose additional losses in personnel, time, and equipment on the opposing force [enemy]; obstacles can be natural, manmade, or a combination of both. (JP 3-15 and FM 2-01.3)	Obstacles, whether natural or manmade, are those elements that impact a force's ability to maneuver and move rapidly through an area (TC 2-33.4). Some examples of obstacles to ground mobility are buildings, mountains, steep slopes, dense forests, rivers, lakes, urban areas, minefields, trenches, certain religious and cultural sites, and wire obstacles (concertina wire, barb wire). (FM 2-01.3) [See Physical Environment: Terrain: Mobility Classification.]
Cover and Concealment	*Cover* is physical protection from bullets, fragments of exploding rounds, flame, nuclear effects, and biological and chemical agents (FM 2-01.3). *Concealment* is protection from observation or surveillance. (JP 1-02)	Cover does not necessarily provide concealment; concealment does not necessarily provide cover. (FM 2-01.3)
Landforms (Sub-Subvariable)	A feature of the earth's surface attributable to natural causes.	Types of terrain predominating the AO (describes more than 60% of the terrain present in the AO).
Vegetation (Sub-Subvariable)	Plant life or total plant cover (as of an area).	Describes the predominant vegetation found in an AO.

(continued)

Table 3-44. Physical environment: terrain (continued)

Subvariable Setting	Setting or Sub-Subvariable Definition	Considerations and Additional Notes
Terrain Complexity (Sub-Subvariable)	Describes the degree to which the terrain imposes significant limitations on observation, maneuver, fires, and intelligence collection.	Complex terrain is a topographical area consisting of an urban center larger than a village and/or of two or more types of restrictive terrain or environmental conditions occupying the same space. (Restrictive terrain or environmental conditions include but are not limited to slope, high altitude, forestation, severe weather, and urbanization.) (FM 7-100.1 and ATTP 3-34.80)
Mobility Classification (Sub-Subvariable)	Describes the degree to which the terrain allows, slows, or hinders movement from place to place in combat formations.	
Subvariable Links: Physical Environment: Weather, Climate; Infrastructure: Construction Pattern, Urban Zones, Urbanized Building Density.		

3-18. The definitions and settings of the "terrain" sub-subvariables of landforms, vegetation, terrain complexity, and mobility classification are depicted in tables 3-45 through 3-48. These subsets define the physical features, circumstances and conditions surrounding and potentially influencing the execution of operations in an AO.

Table 3-45. Terrain: landforms

Definition: A feature of the earth's surface attributable to natural causes. Landforms do not include man-made features, such as canals, ports, and many harbors. Types of terrain predominating the AO (describes more than 60% of the terrain present in the AO).		
Sub-Subvariable Setting	**Setting Definition**	**Considerations and Additional Notes**
Sloped	Sloping landforms consisting of, but not limited to the following types: cliffs, dells, escarpments, glens, gullies, hills, mountains, plains & plateaus, ridges, valleys, and watersheds.	Limitations inherent with specific types of terrain are enforced by observer-controller rules (live), or computer-enforced simulation rules.
Coastal	Coastal landforms consisting of, but not limited to the following types: bays, beaches, cuspate forelands, capes, coves, delta, fjords, lagoons, sounds, spits, or tombolos.	
Fluvial	Riverine or water type landforms consisting of, but not limited to the following types: arroyos, basins, bars, bayous, lakes, levees, marshes, rivers and streams, swamps, waterfalls, watersheds, or combinations of those mentioned.	
Erosion	Erosion type landforms consisting of, but not limited to the following types: canyons, caves, and disposition or eolian landforms.	
Mountain/Glacial	Mountain landforms consisting of, but not limited to the following types: mountain ranges, crevasses, U-shaped valleys, glaciers, hanging valleys, kale deltas, outwash fans, and other types of valley formations.	
Mixed	Two or more of the above categories of landforms comprising over 80% of the available terrain in an AO.	
Subvariable Links: Physical Environment Climate, Terrain (Mobility Classification, Terrain Complexity).		

Table 3-46. Terrain: vegetation

Definition: Plant life or total plant cover (as of an area). Describes the predominant vegetation found in an AO.		
Sub-Subvariable Setting	**Setting Definition**	**Considerations and Additional Notes**
Desert/ Scrub	A variety of trees that have had their growth stunted by soil or climatic conditions. Shrubs comprise the undergrowth in open forests, but in arid and semiarid areas they are the dominant vegetation. Shrubs normally offer no serious obstacle to movement and provide good concealment from ground observation; however, they may restrict fields of fire.	Settings used primarily a virtual or constructive training environment. Can be replicated live in select instances by applying observer-controller-enforced rules to govern behavior in the type of area specified.
Grassland (Tall/Short)	Grasslands from 0.5 to 2 m in height. Grassland more than 1 m high is considered tall. Very tall grass may provide concealment for foot troops. Foot movement in savannah grasslands is slow and tiring; vehicular movement is easy; and observation from the air is easy. Improved solid trafficability during seasonal wet periods.	
Woodlands	Broadleaf, deciduous, or coniferous forests capable of slowing dismounted troops and military vehicles, channelizing movement and causing limited observation and fields of fire. The type of woodland is determined by the dominant tree type (more than 60% of either deciduous or coniferous types). Forests containing less than 60% mix of either type are considered mixed.	
Mixed	Two or more of the above types.	
Subvariable Links: Physical Environment: Climate, Terrain (Mobility Classification, Terrain Complexity).		

Table 3-47. Terrain: terrain complexity

Definition: Describes the degree to which the terrain imposes significant limitations on observation, maneuver, fires, and intelligence collection. Complex terrain is a topographical area consisting of an urban center larger than a village and/or of two or more types of restrictive terrain or environmental conditions occupying the same space. (Restrictive terrain or environmental conditions include but are not limited to slope, high altitude, forestation, severe weather, and urbanization.) (FM 7-100.1 and ATTP 3-34.80)		
Sub-Subvariable Setting	**Setting Definition**	**Considerations and Additional Notes**
Urban Area plus Other Types	An urban area larger than a village occurs in conjunction with of other types of restrictive terrain and/or environmental conditions.	An urban area generally consists of a large central core with a population density of at least 1,000 inhabitants per square mile and adjacent densely settled areas with a population density of at least 500 inhabitants per square mile that together have a total population of at least 2,500. (A village is a small community incorporated as a municipality in a rural area, with a population of 100 to 2,500.)
Urban Area Alone	An urban area larger than a village, in and of itself, constitutes complex terrain—without the presence of other types of restrictive terrain and/or environmental conditions.	
Two or More Types of Restrictive Terrain and/or Environmental Conditions	A combination of two or more types of restrictive terrain (other than urban) and/or environmental conditions.	Restrictive terrain or environmental conditions (other than urbanization) include but are not limited to slope, high altitude, forestation, and severe weather.
Single Type of Restrictive Terrain or Environmental Condition	A single type of restrictive terrain (other than urban) or environmental condition.	
Unrestricted	No urban area or other type of restrictive terrain or environmental condition is present.	Self-explanatory.
Subvariable Links: Infrastructure: Urbanized Building Density; Physical Environment: Climate, Terrain (Landforms, Vegetation, Mobility Classification).		

Table 3-48. Terrain: mobility classification

Definition: Describes the degree to which the terrain allows, slows, or hinders movement from place to place in combat formations.		
Sub-Subvariable Setting	**Setting Definition**	**Considerations and Additional Notes**
Unrestricted Terrain	Terrain that is free of any restriction to movement. Nothing needs to be done to enhance mobility. Unrestricted terrain for armored or mechanized forces is typically flat to moderately sloping terrain with scattered or widely spaced obstacles such as trees or rocks. Unrestricted terrain allows wide maneuver by the forces under consideration and unlimited travel supported by well-developed road networks.	The settings for this sub-subvariable and their definitions come from FM 2-01.3.
Restricted Terrain	Terrain that hinders movement to some degree. Little effort is needed to enhance mobility, but units may have difficulty maintaining preferred speeds, moving in combat formations, or transitioning from one formation to another. Restricted terrain slows movement by requiring zigzagging or frequent detours. Restricted terrain for armored or mechanized forces typically consists of moderate-to-steep slopes or moderate-to-densely spaced obstacles such as trees, rocks, or buildings. Swamps or rugged terrain are examples of restricted terrain for dismounted infantry forces. Logistical or sustainment area movement may be supported by poorly developed road systems.	
Severely Restricted Terrain	Terrain that severely hinders or slows movement in combat formations unless some effort is made to enhance mobility. This could take the form of committing engineer assets to improving mobility or of deviating from doctrinal tactics, such as moving in columns instead of line formations or at speeds much lower than those preferred. Severely restricted terrain for armored and mechanized forces is typically characterized by steep slopes and large or densely spaced obstacles with few or no supporting roads.	
Subvariable Links: Physical Environment: Terrain (Landforms), Weather (Precipitation), Climate.		

NATURAL HAZARDS

3-19. The effects of the "natural hazards" subvariable may involve Army units providing various types of support when conducting humanitarian relief, civil order, or other similar missions. Training for these events can be replicated in simulated settings or by the use of observer-controller enforced rules to govern transit and survivability of such events in a live setting. Definitions of "natural hazards" and the associated subvariable and subvariable setting definitions are listed in table 3-49.

Table 3-49. Physical environment: natural hazards

Definition: Describes the type of natural disasters or hazards that may be encountered when conducting stability or civil support operations.		
Subvariable Setting	**Setting Definition**	**Considerations and Additional Notes**
Volcanic Eruption	Self-explanatory. Characterized by moderate to fast lava flows and possible explosive eruptions of rock and hot ash (similar to the Mt St Helens eruptions and after effects).	Can be replicated in live, virtual, or constructive training environment by the adoption simulated of chemical, nuclear attack conditions (virtual or constructive), or the use of observer-controller-enforced rules to govern transit and survivability of such events in a live training environment.
Drought	A drought is an extended period of months or years when a region notes a deficiency in its water supply. Generally, this occurs when a region receives consistently below average precipitation.	
Tornado	A tornado is a violent, dangerous, rotating column of air which is in contact with both the surface of the earth and a cumulonimbus cloud or, in rare cases, the base of a cumulus cloud. Tornadoes come in many sizes but are typically in the form of a visible condensation funnel, whose narrow end touches the earth and is often encircled by a cloud of debris and dust.	
Monsoon	Monsoon rainfall is considered to be that which occurs in any region that receives the majority of its rain during a particular season.	
Earthquake	Large-magnitude, long-duration, surface quakes resulting in severe infrastructure damage and urban destruction.	
Flooding	Large-area flooding of 2 to 3 m of depth, disrupting all transportation, destroying infrastructure, and subsiding after a prolonged period. Often accompanied by local contagions and waterborne diseases.	
Avalanche	Self-explanatory. Large-scale effect occurring primarily in a mountain or terraced valley.	
Cyclone	A cyclone is a storm system characterized by a large low-pressure center and numerous thunderstorms that produce strong winds, heavy rain and tornados. Depending on its location and strength, a tropical cyclone is referred to by many other names, such as hurricane, typhoon, tropical storm, cyclonic storm, tropical depression, and simply cyclone.	
Other	Any natural, biological, short-term, short-duration, large-area affect, propagated by either weather or prevailing terrain conditions present in an OE. Includes diseases.	
None	Self-explanatory.	
Subvariable Links: Physical Environment: Weather, Climate; Infrastructure: Construction Pattern, Urbanized Building Density.		

CLIMATE

3-20. Climate has profound effects military operations. Training units should be exposed to as many types of climate as possible, simulated or real, especially the type(s) prevalent in those areas they may likely be deployed. Table 3-50 on page 3-38 lists the various types of climates that exist. Understanding their effects on military equipment and soldiers is critical to any successful military operation.

Table 3-50. Physical environment: climate

Definition: Climate is the average course or condition of the weather at a place over a period of years as exhibited by temperature, wind velocity, and precipitation. The type of climate is determined by factors such as latitude, altitude, proportion of land to water, and proximity to oceans and mountains. Climate zones share similar climatic attributes, usually in particular latitudinal distances from the equator.

Subvariable Setting	Setting Definition	Considerations and Additional Notes
Tropical	A type of climate characterized by 12 months of mean temperatures above 18°C (64.4°F) and almost continuous rainfall throughout the year, usually convectional occurring predominantly in the afternoon.	In replicable environments, climate is primarily classified on the basis of temperature and precipitation. Climatic descriptions are used in scenarios to vary climatic conditions to better train units, exposing them to the variety of climatic conditions and their effects on operations. This subvariable is primarily used in a virtual or constructive environment. Some climatic conditions can be replicated in a live environment using scenario-based rules and play box restrictions on training unit and OPFOR movement and actions.
Arid	Climate encountered in regions too dry to support a forest, but not dry enough to be a desert. The soil is considered too moist to be a desert, but too dry to support normal forest life. Characterized by hot summers and cold winters, with 10-20 inches of rain or snowfall per year.	
Mediterranean	A climate that resembles those of the lands bordering the Mediterranean Sea. These climates generally occur on the western coasts of continental landmasses, roughly between the latitudes of 30° and 45° north and south of the equator. Areas with this climate receive almost all of their yearly rainfall during the winter season, and may go anywhere from 2-5 months during the summer without having any significant precipitation.	
Oceanic	Oceanic climates are characterized by a narrower annual range of temperatures than are encountered in other places at a comparable latitude, and differ from Mediterranean climates in that significant amounts of precipitation are received in summer.	
Continental	Characterized by winter temperatures cold enough to support a fixed period of stable snow cover each year, and relatively low precipitation occurring mostly in summer, although east coast areas (chiefly in North America) may show an even distribution of precipitation. They have either forest or tall-grass prairie as natural ground covers and include some of the most productive farmlands in the world. All such climates have at least 3 months of temperatures in excess of 10°C (50°F) and winters with at least one month below 0°C (32°F).	
Subarctic	Characterized by long, usually very cold winters and brief, warm summers. It is found on large landmasses in the Northern Hemisphere, away from the moderating effects of an ocean, generally at latitudes from 50°N to 70°N (immediately south of the true arctic). Temperatures can drop to -40°C (also -40°F) in winter and may exceed 30°C (86°F) in summer. However, the summers are short, no more than 3 months of the year (but at least 1 month) and must have a 24-hour average temperature of at least 10°C (50°F) to fall in this category.	

Subvariable Links: Physical Environment: Weather, Natural Hazards.

WEATHER

3-21. Definitions of "weather" and the associated sub-subvariables are listed in table 3-51. Weather should not be confused with climate. *Weather* refers to the activity or atmospheric condition at a given time or over shorter periods up to approximately two weeks, while *climate* refers to the average course or condition of these same elements over a period of years.

Table 3-51. Physical environment: weather

Definition: Weather is a set of all the phenomena occurring in a given atmosphere at a given time. Weather phenomena lie in the hydrosphere and troposphere.

Sub-Subvariable	Sub-Subvariable Definition	Considerations and Additional Notes
Precipitation	Any visible moisture that falls from the atmosphere, such as rain, sleet, snow, hail, drizzle or a combination of these.	Precipitation may be used by exercise control (EXCON) to manage various aspects of an exercise such as rate of advance and visibility.
High Temperature— Heat Index	The measurement of how hot or cold the air is. The heat index (HI) combines air temperature and relative humidity which helps determine the human perceived equivalent temperature.	Knowing the HI in an AO is an important factor in deployments as well as and live and simulated training exercises.
Low Temperature— Wind Chill Index	The measurement of how cold the air is. The Wind-Chill Index combines air temperature and wind speed which helps determine the cooling effect of wind on bare flesh when first exposed.	Knowing the Wind Chill Index in an AO is an important factor in deployments as well as simulated exercises training exercises.
Wind	Air which is in horizontal or near horizontal motion.	
Visibility	The mean distance at which the naked eye can see prominent objects through the atmosphere.	Accurate timing based upon available light is critical in planning military operations. It is expressed in the number of degrees the center of the sun is below the horizon. Although technically not weather data, it is customarily considered together with weather factors because both affect visibility such as cloud cover. Light is also a critical factor in the employment of light sensitive equipment such as night vision and thermal devices.
Cloud Cover	The amount of clouds over or at a given location.	Cloud cover may be used by exercise control (EXCON) to manage various aspects of an exercise such as flight operations and visibility.
Relative Humidity	Humidity is the term used to describe the amount of water vapor in the air. The amount of water vapor the air actually contains compared with the maximum it can hold at a given temperature and pressure is termed the relative humidity of the air.	

Subvariable Links: Physical Environment: Climate, Natural Hazards.

3-22. The definitions and settings of the "weather" sub-subvariables of precipitation, high temperature-heat index, low temperature-wind chill index, wind, visibility, cloud cover and relative humidity are depicted in tables 3-52 through 3-58. These subsets define the atmospheric conditions surrounding and potentially influencing the execution of operations in an AO.

Table 3-52. Weather: precipitation

Definition: Any visible moisture that falls from the atmosphere, such as rain, sleet, snow, hail, drizzle or a combination of these. Precipitation occurs when the atmosphere, a large gaseous solution becomes saturated with water vapor and the water condenses and descends from the solution (that is, precipitates).

Sub-Subvariable Setting	Setting Definition	Considerations and Additional Notes
Very light	Scattered drops or flakes that do not completely wet an exposed surface regardless of duration.	
Light	A trace of .10 inch of precipitation per hour with a maximum of .01 inch in 6 minutes.	
Moderate	.11 to .30 inch per hour; between .01 and .03 inch in 6 minutes.	
Heavy	More than .30 inch per hour; more than .03 inch in 6 minutes.	

Subvariable Links: Physical Environment: Climate, Natural Hazards.

Table 3-53. Weather: high temperature—heat index

Definition: The measurement of how hot or cold the air is. Temperature is measured with thermometers that may be calibrated to a variety of temperature scales. Since the majority of military operations will most likely be in areas of moderate to extreme heat, a more useful measurement is heat index (HI). The HI combines air temperature and relative humidity which helps determine the human perceived equivalent temperature.

Sub-Subvariable Setting	Setting Definition	Considerations and Additional Notes
75-85°F	**Caution** – Fatigue is possible with prolonged exposure and activity. Continuing activity could result in heat camps and nausea.	Understanding the average temperatures and HI in an AO is an important factor in deployments as well as and live-, virtual-, and gaming-based training exercises.
85-105°F	**Extreme Caution** – Use extreme caution in any prolonged physical activity. Continuing activity could result in heat exhaustion or heat stroke.	
95-130°F	**Danger** – heat cramps and heat exhaustion are highly possible. Continued activity could result in heat stroke.	
Over 130°F	**Extreme Danger** – heat stroke is imminent with any continuing activity.	

Subvariable Links: Physical Environment: Climate, Natural Hazards.

Table 3-54. Weather: low temperature—wind chill index

Definition: The measurement of how cold the air is. Temperature is measured with thermometers that may be calibrated to a variety of temperature scales. Some military operations will include areas of moderate to extreme cold, for which a more useful measurement is Wind-Chill Index. Wind-Chill Index combines air temperature and wind speed which helps determine the cooling effect of wind on bare flesh when first exposed.

Sub-Subvariable Setting	Setting Definition	Considerations and Additional Notes
From wind speed of 1 mph at 50°F to 40 mph at 20°F	**Minimal Danger** – Exposed flesh may freeze within 60 minutes. However, this range is also very dangerous because it gives a false sense of security.	The cooling effect is the same whether the human body is moving through the air or the air is blowing past the body. The effect of wind will be less if a person has even slight protection for exposed parts, such as light gloves on hands, or parka hood shielding face. Wind speeds greater than 40 mph have little additional effect. Understanding the average temperatures and current Wind-Chill Index in an AO is an important factor in deployments as well as and live-, virtual-, and gaming-based training exercises.
From 1 mph at -30°F to 40 mph at -10°F	**Increasing Danger** – Danger from freezing of exposed flesh within 60 seconds.	
From 10 mph at -50°F to 40 mph at -60°F	**Great Danger** – Danger from freezing of exposed flesh within 30 seconds.	

Subvariable Links: Physical Environment: Climate, Natural Hazards.

Table 3-55. Weather: wind

Definition: Air which is in horizontal or near horizontal motion. Vertical movements of air are known as air current and are caused by differences in density between two air masses. Wind direction is determined by the direction from which it is blowing.

Sub-Subvariable Setting	Setting Definition	Considerations and Additional Notes
Calm	**Less than 1 mph**; smoke rises vertically.	Setting names, wind speeds and effects are all based on the Beaufort Scale.
Moderate Breeze	**13-18 mph**; raises dust, loose paper, small branches are moved.	Wind effects such as speed and direction are critical in all military operations but especially in the use of chemical agents, concealment, observation, and smoke obscuration.
Strong Breeze	**25-31 mph**; large branches in motion; whistling heard in above-ground electrical wires, umbrellas used with difficulty.	
Moderate Gale	**32-38 mph**; whole trees in motion; difficulty walking against the wind.	
Strong Gale	**47-54 mph**; slight structural damage occurs (chimney and roofing damaged).	
Storm	**56-63 mph**; unable to walk, widespread structural damage.	

Subvariable Links: Physical Environment: Climate, Natural Hazards.

Table 3-56. Weather: visibility

Definition: The mean distance at which the naked eye can see prominent objects through the atmosphere.

(Accurate timing based upon available light is critical in planning military operations. It is expressed in the number of degrees the center of the sun is below the horizon. Although technically not weather data, it is customarily considered together with weather factors because both affect visibility such as cloud cover. Light is also a critical factor in the employment of light sensitive equipment such as night vision and thermal devices.)

Sub-Subvariable Setting	Setting Definition	Considerations and Additional Notes
Beginning of Morning Nautical Twilight (BMNT)	Before sunrise, when the sun is 12 degrees below the horizon. Illumination is poor, and only vague outlines are visible.	An important visibility consideration called thermal (IR) crossover occurs, depending on the cloud ceiling, soon after BMNT and EENT. Thermal crossover occurs when the temperature of a target is the same as the temperature of its background. When this occurs, targets will appear invisible to IR sensors.
Beginning of Morning Civil Twilight (BMCT)	Before sunrise, when the sun is 6 degrees below the horizon. On a clear day, outdoor activity is visible.	Under ideal conditions, the period of time when there is adequate visibility for large-scale operations is between BMNT and EECT. Generally, visibility at BMNT is about 400 m, which is enough light for close coordination between personnel.
End of Evening Civil Twilight (EECT)	After sunset, when the sun is 6 degrees below the horizon. On a clear day, outdoor activity is visible.	Halfway between EECT and EENT (or BMNT and BMCT), there is enough light for visual ground adjustment of close-in artillery fire and air strikes.
End of Evening Nautical Twilight (EENT)	After sunset, when the sun is 12 degrees below the horizon. Illumination is poor, and only vague outlines are visible.	

Subvariable Links: Physical Environment: Climate, Natural Hazards.

Table 3-57. Weather: cloud cover

Definition: The amount of clouds over or at a given location.		
Sub-Subvariable Setting	**Setting Definition**	**Considerations and Additional Notes**
Clear	No clouds or less than 1/8 of the sky is covered.	Cloud conditions are expressed as cloud bases or ceiling in which the amount of cover is stated in eighths. Several layers of scattered clouds added together may result in a broken or overcast condition. Low clouds impact many battlefield operations, especially the use of smart weapons (TC 2-33.4).
Scattered	1/8 to 4/8 of the sky is covered, inclusive.	
Broken	5/8 to 7/8 of the sky is covered, inclusive.	
Overcast	8/8 (100%) of the sky is covered.	
Subvariable Links: Physical Environment: Climate, Natural Hazards.		

Table 3-58. Weather: relative humidity

Definition: Humidity is the term used to describe the amount of water vapor in the air. The amount of water vapor the air actually contains compared with the maximum it can hold at a given temperature and pressure is termed the relative humidity of the air. Relative humidity is an important metric used in forecasting weather. Humidity indicates the likelihood of precipitation, dew, or fog. High humidity makes soldiers feel hotter outside in the summer because it reduces the effectiveness of sweating to cool the body by preventing the evaporation or perspiration from the skin. An accurate measurement of this effect is called the Wet-Bulb-Glove-Temperature (WBGT) Index, which is calculated using a combination of temperature, humidity and wind. WBGT reports are obtained from supporting combat medical units.		
Sub-Subvariable Setting	**Setting Definition**	**Considerations and Additional Notes**
WBGT index reaches 78°F	Extremely intense physical exertion may precipitate heat exhaustion or heat stroke. Caution should be taken.	Add 10° to all measured WBGTs when Soldiers are wearing body armor or CBRN warfare clothing.
WBGT index reaches 85°F	Strenuous exercise, such as marching in standard cadence should be stopped for unseasoned Soldiers during their first 3 weeks in the AO.	
WBGT index reaches 88°F	Strenuous exercise should be stopped for all Soldiers with less than 12 weeks of training in hot weather.	
WBGT index reaches 90°F	Physical training and strenuous exercise should be stopped for all Soldiers.	This does not apply to critical operational commitments where the risk of heat casualties may be warranted. However, hydration and sun cover are extremely important.
Subvariable Links: Physical Environment: Climate.		

TIME VARIABLE

3-23. The Time variable describes the timing and duration of activities, events, or conditions that occur, exist, or continue within an OE, as well as how the timing and duration are perceived by various actors in the OE. Various aspects of time and the perception of them can affect and influence military operations (friendly and enemy) within an OE. They can affect the reasons for conducting an operation, the amount of time available to complete a mission, the duration of an operation, and how commanders employ forces to achieve conditions of the desired end state. Different groups of people may perceive the concept of time in different ways. The perception and experience of time are among the most central aspects of how groups function and interact. In a military context, time orientation affects decision cycles, planning horizons, and tempo of operations.

3-24. The specific Time subvariables and their settings depicted in table 3-59 represent replicable conditions that may be present within an OE for a training exercise. Their associated definitions, considerations, additional notes, and external links are listed separately in tables 3-60 through 3-65.

Table 3-59. Time variable and subvariable settings

Variable	Time					
Subvariable	Knowledge of the AO	Cultural Percep-tion of Time	Key-Event Resolution	Information Offset	Tactical Exploitation of Time	Key Dates, Time Periods, or Events
Subvariable Settings	Entry	Not Time Sensitive	Low	Low	Low	Traditional Wed-ding Season
	Established	Medium	Medium	Medium	Medium	Secular or Religious Holi-days
	Exit	High	High	High	High	Anniversary of Historical Incidents
						Elections
						Natural Disasters
						Agricultural Crop/Livestock Market Cycles

Table 3-60. Time: knowledge of the AO

Definition: Defines the amount of knowledge that the training unit would rightfully possess based on the amount of time the unit has spent in the AO prior to scenario STARTEX.		
Subvariable Setting	Setting Definition	Considerations and Additional Notes
Entry	Training unit is initially beginning its tour of duty. The unit is not established and has limited knowledge of the AO.	The range of settings determines the amount of information offset that the training unit and OPFOR are entitled to prior to the exercise.
Established	Training unit is mid-way through its deployment. The unit is established and has a moderate knowledge of the AO.	Time is equal to both friendly and enemy. Any information offset (for the training unit) should also be matched by appropriate behaviors for the OPFOR. For example, if the training unit has 3 months to prepare the OPFOR has the same 3 months to enhance defenses and maneuver, as well as acquire additional resources, men, and equipment.
Exit	Training unit is nearing the end of its deploy-ment in the AO. The unit is established and has detailed knowledge of the AO.	
Subvariable Links: Information: Intelligence; Time: Key-Event Resolution, Information Offset.		

Table 3-61. Time: cultural perception of time

Definition: The cultural perception of time is one of the most important aspects of how different people groups function and interact. Cultural awareness includes sensitivity to how a given culture in the AO perceives the concept of time. Cultural understanding of time can be used as an operational planning factor and a tool to manipulate tactical and strategic advantages.

Subvariable Setting	Setting Definition	Considerations and Additional Notes
Not Time Sensitive	Enemy views a protracted conflict as an advantage. May view a long-term conflict as a key objective.	For CTC replication, role-players should reflect appropriate cultural perception of time. If different than the U.S. perception, it should be reflected in the scenario.
Medium	Enemy views a protracted conflict as a possible advantage. May show flexibility in their ability to change their view of timeliness based on how the conflict unfolds.	
High	Enemy views a protracted conflict as a liability and not to their advantage. May view a timely resolution of the conflict as a key objective.	

Subvariable Links: Social: Ethnic Diversity, Education Level; Time: Key Dates, Time Periods, or Events.

Table 3-62. Time: key-event resolution

Definition: The number of key events and related orders of effect designed into the scenario in order to accomplish unit training objectives. The setting may describe the entire scenario, including sub-events or may describe specific key events within the scenario.

Subvariable Setting	Setting Definition	Considerations and Additional Notes
Low	1-3 OE key events planned with sufficient planning conducted to execute effects in response to probable training unit actions. Key-events effects depth limited to 2nd-order effects. Setting used for a relatively inexperienced unit to emphasize specific training objectives.	Decision on which setting should be selected is based on the commander's training assessment of the unit and key exercise decisions made in phase 1 of the exercise design sequence. (See chapter 2.)
Medium	4-5 OE key events planned with sufficient planning conducted to execute effects in response to probable training unit actions. Key-event effects depth limited to 3rd-order effects. Setting used for a trained, moderately experienced unit.	
High	10-12 OE key events planned with sufficient planning conducted to execute effects in response to probable training unit actions. Key-event effects depth expanded to capture 2nd-, 3rd-, and 4th-order effects in response to training unit actions and counter-actions. Setting used only for a highly experienced, capable unit.	

Sub variable Links: Time: Knowledge of the AO, Information Offset.

Table 3-63. Time: Information offset

Definition: Tips, informants, and serendipitous events or reports that presage OPFOR activities in a meaningful, predictive way.

Subvariable Setting	Setting Definition	Considerations and Additional Notes
Low	10% of all OPFOR activities or key events are presaged by sufficient tips, hints, or indicators to enable successful training unit reaction or interdiction to the events.	This information is either provided to the training unit prior to STARTEX for planning purposes or is scripted into the scenario.
Medium	20% of all OPFOR activities or key events are presaged by sufficient tips, hints, or indicators to enable successful training unit reaction or interdiction to the events.	
High	30% of all OPFOR activities or key events are presaged by sufficient tips, hints, or indicators to enable successful training unit reaction or interdiction to the events.	

Subvariable Links: Time: Key-Event Resolution, Knowledge of the AO.

Table 3-64. Time: tactical exploitation of time

Definition: The ability of the enemy to use time for tactical advantage. Examples of events used to gain or manipulate time to the enemy's advantage are—
- **Delay** (trade space for time). Could be as simple as delaying or destroying MEDEVAC or interrupting the information flow or decision cycle. Attack to delay is an accepted method as is swarming (mobs) by civilians to delay and disrupt.
- **Deception** (lead enemy in different direction or focus).
- **Fix** (forces, obstacles, mines, etc.).
- **Block** (forces, obstacles, mines, CBRN, etc.).

Subvariable Setting	Setting Definition	Considerations and Additional Notes
Low	Enemy can conduct limited operations designed to manipulate time against small-unit tactical forces. Generally, friendly forces fall prey to "basic" opportunistic traps. Enemy has limited knowledge of the OE.	Decision on which setting should be selected is based on the commander's training assessment of the unit and key exercise decisions made in phase 1 of the exercise design sequence. (See chapter 2.)
Medium	Enemy is adept at using time to advantage against regular forces and infantry. Enemy has a moderate knowledge of the OE and friendly TTP and locations.	
High	Enemy is very adept at using time to advantage at all levels in all conditions. Enemy has a detailed knowledge of the OE and friendly TTP and locations.	

Subvariable Links: Military: Military Forces; Information: Intelligence; Time: Knowledge of the AO; Information Offset.

Table 3-65. Time: key dates, time periods, or events

Definition: Routine, cyclical, planned, unplanned key dates, time periods, or events that significantly affect organizations, people, and military operations. Templating of these events is vital to establish or maintain control and predict future events. Once key dates, time periods, or events are determined, it is important to template the events and to analyze them for their impact on current or future military operations.

Subvariable Setting (Examples)	Setting Definition	Considerations and Additional Notes
Traditional Wedding Season	Traditional times during the year when weddings occur.	Other considerations are how and where these events are celebrated. For example, in many Asian nations wedding parties light fireworks or fire weapons in the air in harmless celebration.
Secular or Religious Holidays	Self-explanatory.	An example of military consideration would be country X where Christmas is not celebrated by 95% of population. The 5% of Christians and Christian Churches may require additional security.
Anniversary of Historical Incidents	Special milestone to be celebrated which is not necessarily routine or a cyclical, routine event.	An example would be the 200th birthday of a significant political or religious leader, which may be controversial among certain ethnic groups within a population.
Elections	Political elections including local, regional, and levels. Includes primary and general elections as well as scheduled and special elections.	May be a very critical time for a country and its future security. May require high security, especially if the outcome is significant, the country has a track record of widespread voter fraud, or the election includes the participation of first-time voter minorities.
Natural Disasters	Disasters created by catastrophic weather or environmental events.	Natural disasters affect the attitudes and activities of government and civilian populations. These changes cause stress in the civilian population and its leaders. Addressing the problems posed by disasters requires considerable time and resources.
Agricultural Crop/Livestock Market Cycles	Seasonal periods when harvest or significant livestock sales occur.	During these periods, a significant increase in road traffic of slow-moving vehicles occurs. Impact can be significant on military major or secondary supply routes.

Subvariable Links: Social: Ethnic Diversity; Physical Environment: Natural Hazards; Time: Cultural Perception of Time.

Appendix A

Exercise Design Checklist

The Exercise Design Checklist (table A-1) is a sequential, summarized list of key exercise design tasks and associated events as described in phases 1 through 4 in chapter 2. These include exercise parameters; task and countertask development; PMESII-PT OE development; orders, plans, and instructions; and typical briefings, conferences, and control documents. The righthand column contains page references in this TC for each step/task and action required. This checklist is not intended to be all-inclusive but rather to provide those critical tasks that must be accomplished within the design process. As noted in chapter 2, depending on the type of exercise and available OE information, certain tasks may occur in different phases.

Table A-1. Exercise design checklist

Design Phase	Step/Task	Action Required	Additional Notes	Pages
Phase 1: Initial Planning	Define exercise parameters.	Developed based on commander's training assessment and exercise director's initial guidance, troop list, unit training objectives (METL), requested conditions and resources. Product is defined exercise parameters and prioritized training objectives (METL).	Depending on the type and size of the exercise event, an initial planning conference may be required. This is normally the first meeting between the senior trainer, exercise director, and exercise planner.	2-2 and 2-3
	Determine exercise time-line.	Consider amount of time available, training objectives, training support personnel required, and available transportation and training facilities.	If time is limited, training objectives may have to be modified or eliminated in order to compensate for this shortfall.	2-3
	Determine whether exercise will be live, virtual, constructive, gaming, or a combination.	Refer to exercise parameters to determine resources to support live, virtual, constructive or gaming training event.	Consider aspects such as troops available, equipment status, and geographical space.	2-3 and 2-4
	Determine operational theme.	Refer to proposed training objectives, requested conditions and the exercise director's initial guidance.	Depending on the time allotted and the experience of the training unit, it may be possible to train sequentially under two different themes.	2-4
	Determine whether using existing or composite OE.	Selection will depend on the type of mission, training resources and availability of OE data.	In almost all cases, training exercises will contain portions of existing, modified, or composite OEs.	2-4

Phase 2: Task and Countertask Development	Determine OPFOR countertasks.	Using the prioritized training objectives (METL), exercise parameters, and OPFOR UTL, select those OPFOR countertasks in order to counter and stress the training unit.	Refer to appendix B, OPFOR tactical task list for selection of appropriate tasks keeping in mind resources available and the desired fidelity of the exercise.	2-5 thru 2-7
	Develop OPFOR OB and task organization.	Using the selected OPFOR countertasks and FM 7-100.4, develop OPFOR OB and build the appropriate task organization.	As discussed in chapter 2, this particular step will depend on whether there is an existing OE and associated OB. If so, this step may not be necessary or may occur in later phases.	2-7 thru 2-9
	Select OPFOR tier levels.	Using the selected OPFOR task-organized unit, select the appropriate WEG tier levels. Product is a fully developed OPFOR unit.	Same as above. Note that most OPFOR units should have a mix of various tier levels in order to provide more realistic training.	2-9 thru 2-11
Phase 3: PMESII-PT OE Development	Develop the OE.	Using the PMESII-PT variables, select the appropriate subvariable settings listed in chapter 3 to produce the training conditions that support the training tasks required.	As is the case with developing the OPFOR, this step is also dependent on whether there is an existing OE. If this is an MRX for a real-world mission, the OE normally exists already. Whether using existing OE or composite, the exercise planner should go through all the variables and their subvariables to ensure the entire conditions are set for the training objectives.	2-12 thru 2-16
		Chapter 2 provides an example of one logical flow of the sequence for consideration of PMESII-PT variables.	This sequence is situation dependent, and the example may not work in all cases. Planners are not restricted to this particular selection sequence.	2-16 thru 2-19
	Refine supporting METL tasks and associated task organization.	Using the OE-WFF analysis matrix depicted in chapter 2, examine whether or not the proposed supporting METL tasks and task organization are still accurate based on the defined OE.	Regardless of whether or not there is a real OE, planners should review the supporting tasks against the OE and WFF to ensure all tasks and task organization are accurate or need to be modified prior to STARTEX.	2-19 thru 2-21
	Determine common processes for the desired OE.	Preplanned events that represent everyday activities common to all exercise OEs.	The level of fidelity of key events and the number of variables and subvariables replicated will be determined by factors such as the experience level of the training unit, the type of training exercise, and the number of role-players available.	2-21 and 2-22

	Determine key events to highlight chosen training objectives.	With the guidance from the senior trainer and exercise director, select key events that are preprogrammed into the existing or developed OE that will result in training value for the unit.	Indicators can build up to a key event, and a key event can result in 2nd-, 3rd-, and even 4th-order effects.	2-22
Phase 4: Orders, Plans, and Instruction Development	Prepare and conduct final exercise planning conference.	Exercise planner presents an overview of the entire exercise to ensure all details are complete. Senior trainer, EXCON, OPFOR commander, exercise director, and the training unit commander normally attend.	Results of this final planning conference lock in all exercise parameters, which include troop lists, training objectives, and the exercise OE. Includes final review and approval or disapproval of unit requests for equipment and troop list exceptions outside the normal TOE.	2-23
	Prepare and conduct final exercise briefing.	Exercise planner provides the final pre-exercise information briefing to the exercise director and all pertinent staff. Normally conducted 30 days from STARTEX.	The briefing covers all aspects of the exercise. No decisions are expected except for deconfliction on any last-minute issues. Briefing includes disposition of forces, chronology of key events, and C-, M-, and D-Day.	2-23 and 2-24
	Develop and issue higher unit warning orders, intelligence estimates and other exercise documents to the training unit.	Exercise director may direct exercise planner to develop and issue various documents and plans to the player unit. These may include warning orders, country studies and intelligence summaries.	These documents are issued in order to promote realism in training and provide information to the player unit prior to the exercise. This information allows training units to develop preparatory home station training prior to the actual exercise.	2-24
	Develop and issue higher unit OPLANs and orders to the training unit.	Exercise planner will develop higher unit OPLANs and orders to initiate the training unit's mission planning cycle and orders development process.	These documents provide key planning information. Combined with the above documents, they enable the training unit to conduct its internal mission planning and orders production process.	2-24
	Develop and issue OPFOR orders.	Using the OPFOR counter-tasks, OB, and defined OE, the exercise planner develops and issues OPFOR orders.	These documents provide key planning information. They enable the OPFOR unit to conduct its internal mission planning and rehearsal process.	2-24 and 2-25
	Develop instructions for role-players.	Using the COE Actors and Role-Players Handbook, the exercise planner develops role-player instructions in order to support exercise realism, common processes, key events, and the selected OE subvariables. Provides specific acting and material guidance to role-players so that they accurately represent the desired training conditions.	Instructions are normally sent out NLT 30 days prior to STARTEX. The document describes the exercise OE and its relationship to role-player requirements, and includes scenario timeline and areas to be occupied (who, what, where, when, and duration) as well as personal and group profiles.	2-25 thru 2-27

	Develop and issue the road to war to the training unit.	Using all products developed in phases 1 through 4, the exercise planner develops and issues the road to war.	This document is normally the last document produced in the exercise design sequence because it depends on other products in order to be completed. It is a historical document that normally explains the chronology of events that has produced the current situation. It should include the deployment and disposition of the training unit and OPFOR units at STARTEX; identify C-Day, M-Day, and D-Day; and provide reasoning for the execution of training objectives and subtasks.	2-27

OPFOR Tactical Task List

The OPFOR Tactical Task List is a listing of tactical tasks that are specific to the OPFOR. OPFOR tactical organizations and individuals perform these tasks instead of the comparable tasks in the Army Universal Task List (AUTL). OPFOR organizations and individuals perform tactical tasks in order to provide challenging conditions for the execution or attempted execution of mission essential tasks by training units.

B-1. The OPFOR Tactical Task List serves as the primary source for most tasks the OPFOR must perform. Exercise planners reference this list first when conducting countertask analysis. Only if the OPFOR Tactical Task List does not contain an appropriate task is one selected for the OPFOR from the AUTL.

B-2. The format of providing the OPFOR Tactical Task List will be to first define the tactical task and then list its subtasks (and in some cases, sub-subtasks). This will be followed by a table which shows the associated measures of performance for the overall task (or for major subtasks that have sub-subtasks). Each tactical task will numbered in order to provide a standard reference for easier identification.

TACTICAL TASK 1.0 ASSAULT

B-3. An *assault* is an attack that destroys an enemy force through firepower and the physical occupation and/or destruction of his position. An assault is the basic form of OPFOR tactical offensive combat. Assaults at any level of command and with any type forces have the same basic subtasks:

- **1.1 Isolate**
  - Maneuver and deploy security element(s) to ensure additional enemy forces do not join the battle unexpectedly. (Security elements may become fixing elements.)
  - Continue to provide early warning.
  - Prevent the enemy from gaining further information.
  - Prevent enemy maneuver.
- **1.2 Suppress**
  - Provide lethal and nonlethal suppression.
  - Suppress the enemy force to permit the assault element to move against the enemy position without receiving destructive fire.
- **1.3 Assault**
  - From the direction where least return fire is possible, the assault element employs surprise, limited visibility, complex terrain, and camouflage, concealment, cover, and deception (C3D) to attain the enemy position while remaining combat effective.
  - Maneuver to and seize the enemy position, destroying any forces there.

TACTICAL TASK 1.0 ASSAULT		
No.	Scale	Measure
01	Yes/No	Unit isolates enemy from assistance.
02	Time	To suppress enemy.
03	Time	To execute assault.
04	Yes/No	Enemy position seized.
05	Percent	Of friendly forces available to continue mission.
06	Percent	Combat effectiveness of enemy forces.

TACTICAL TASK 2.0 RAID

B-4. A *raid* is an attack against a stationary target for the purposes of its capture or destruction that culminates in the withdrawal of the raiding detachment to safe territory. Raids can also be used to secure information and to confuse or deceive the enemy. The keys to the successful accomplishment of any are raid surprise, firepower, and violence. The raid ends with a planned withdrawal upon completion of the assigned mission. The subtasks for a raid are—

- **2.1 Infiltrate**
  - Conduct undetected movement through and/or into an area occupied by enemy forces to occupy a position of advantage.
- **2.2 Isolate**
  - Maneuver and deploy security element(s) to ensure additional enemy forces do not join the battle unexpectedly. (Security elements may become fixing elements.)
  - Continue to provide early warning.
  - Prevent the enemy from gaining further information.
  - Prevent enemy maneuver.
- **2.3 Seize or Destroy**
  - Attack to destroy or seize personnel or equipment.
  - **2.4 Exfiltrate**
  - Conduct undetected movement from areas under enemy control by stealth, deception, surprise, or clandestine means.

TACTICAL TASK 2.0 RAID		
No.	Scale	Measure
01	Yes/No	Unit infiltrates without detection.
02	Yes/No	Unit isolates enemy from assistance.
03	Time	To seize or destroy raid target.
04	Time	To extract/exfiltrate.
05	Percent	Of friendly forces available to continue mission.

TACTICAL TASK 3.0 AMBUSH (ANNIHILATION)

B-5.   An *ambush* is a surprise attack from a concealed position, used against moving or temporarily halted targets. The purpose of an annihilation ambush is to destroy the enemy force. These are violent attacks designed to ensure the enemy's return fire, if any, is ineffective. Generally, this type of ambush uses the terrain to the attacker's advantage and employs mines and other obstacles to halt the enemy in the kill zone. The goal of the obstacles is to keep the enemy in the kill zone throughout the action. The subtasks for an annihilation ambush are—

- **3.1 Occupy Ambush Site**
- **3.2 Isolate Kill Zone**
  - Maneuver and deploy security element(s) to ensure additional enemy forces do not join the battle unexpectedly. (Security elements may become fixing elements.)
  - Continue to provide early warning.
  - Prevent the enemy from gaining further information.
  - Prevent enemy maneuver.
- **3.3 Contain Enemy**
  - Stop, hold, or surround enemy forces and prevent them from withdrawing any element for use elsewhere.
- **3.4 Destroy**
  - Render the enemy combat ineffective and/or damage selected element(s) of his combat system to the point of uselessness.
- **3.5 Exfiltrate**
  - Conduct undetected movement from areas under enemy control by stealth, deception, surprise, or clandestine means.

TACTICAL TASK 3.0 AMBUSH (ANNIHILATION)		
No.	**Scale**	**Measure**
01	Yes/No	Unit moves to and occupies ambush site without detection.
02	Yes/No	Unit isolates kill zone from assistance.
03	Time	To execute ambush.
04	Yes/No	Enemy in kill zone during projected time window.
05	Yes/No	Enemy contained in kill zone.
06	Percent	Friendly forces available to continue mission.
07	Percent	Combat effectiveness of enemy force.

TACTICAL TASK 4.0 RECONNAISSANCE ATTACK

B-6. A *reconnaissance attack* is a tactical offensive action that locates moving, dispersed, or concealed enemy elements and either fixes or destroys them. It may also be used to gain information. The reconnaissance attack may involve multiple security and assault elements. The subtasks for a reconnaissance attack are—

- **4.1 Find**
  - Employ reconnaissance element(s) to locate target systems or units.
- **4.2 Isolate**
  - Maneuver and deploy security element(s) to ensure additional enemy forces do not join the battle unexpectedly. (Security elements may become fixing elements.)
  - Continue to provide early warning.
  - Prevent enemy maneuver.
  - Prevent the enemy from gaining further information.
- **4.3 Fix**
  - Prevent the enemy from moving any part of his force from a specific location for a specific period of time.
  - The security element(s) making contact fix the enemy. (Security elements become fixing elements.)
  - Security element(s) continue to provide early warning of approaching enemy forces and prevent them from gaining further information on the rest of the OPFOR force.
- **4.4 Destroy**
  - Render the enemy combat ineffective and/or damage selected element(s) of his combat system to the point of uselessness.

TACTICAL TASK 4.0 RECONNAISSANCE ATTACK		
No.	**Scale**	**Measure**
01	Percent	Of enemy elements requiring destruction found.
02	Yes/No	Enemy elements isolated from outside assistance.
03	Time	To find and destroy enemy elements.
04	Percent	Of friendly forces available to continue mission.
05	Percent	Combat effectiveness of enemy force.

TACTICAL TASK 5.0 RECONNAISSANCE

B-7. *Reconnaissance* represents all measures associated with organizing, collecting, and studying information on the enemy, terrain, and weather in the area of upcoming battles. The subtasks for a reconnaissance are—

- **5.1 Fix Enemy Security Forces**
  - Prevent the enemy from moving any part of his security force from a specific location for a specific period of time.
  - The security element(s) making contact fix the enemy. (Security elements become fixing elements.)
  - Security element(s) continue to provide early warning of approaching enemy forces and prevent them from gaining further information on the rest of the OPFOR force.

- **5.2 Find**
  - Employ reconnaissance element(s) to locate selected reconnaissance targets.
- **5.3 Contact**
  - Gain sensor contact between reconnaissance element(s) and their designated reconnaissance target(s).
- **5.4 Report**
  - Provide accurate information on reconnaissance targets in a timely manner.

TACTICAL TASK 5.0 RECONNAISSANCE		
No.	**Scale**	**Measure**
01	Percent	Of reconnaissance targets found.
02	Percent	Of reconnaissance elements able to contact targets.
03	Time	To find and report on all reconnaissance targets.
04	Percent	Of friendly forces available to continue mission.

TACTICAL TASK 6.0 COUNTERRECONNAISSANCE

B-8. *Counterreconnaissance* (CR) is a continuous combined arms action to locate, track and destroy all enemy reconnaissance operating in a given AOR. CR is conducted at all times and during all types of operations. The subtasks for CR are—

- **6.1 Predict**
  - Determine likely types and locations of critical enemy reconnaissance elements.
- **6.2 Find**
  - Employ reconnaissance elements to locate enemy reconnaissance elements.
- **6.3 Report**
  - Provide accurate information on reconnaissance targets in a timely manner.
- **6.4 Neutralize**
  - Destroy, deceive, or obscure enemy reconnaissance elements.

TACTICAL TASK 6.0 COUNTERRECONNAISSANCE		
No.	**Scale**	**Measure**
01	Percent	Of enemy reconnaissance elements found.
02	Percent	Of enemy reconnaissance elements unable to contact targets.
03	Time	To find and report on all critical enemy reconnaissance elements.

TACTICAL TASK 7.0 DEFEND FROM SIMPLE BATTLE POSITION

B-9. A *simple battle position* (SBP) is a defensive location oriented on the most likely enemy avenue of approach or objective area. SBPs are not necessarily tied to restrictive terrain but will employ as much engineer effort as possible to restrict enemy maneuver. Defenders of SBPs will take all actions necessary to prevent enemy penetration of their position, or defeat a penetration once it has occurred. Unlike a complex battle position, which is typically independent, an SBP may form a larger integrated defense with other SBPs. The subtasks for defense from a SBP are—

- **7.1 Control**
  - Orient on enemy avenue of approach.
- **7.2 Gain Advantage**
  - Employ terrain, survivability, and C3D to provide an advantage over attackers.

TACTICAL TASK 7.0 DEFEND FROM SIMPLE BATTLE POSITION		
No.	**Scale**	**Measure**
01A	Yes/No	Attacking enemy force destroyed/position retained.
01B	Yes/No	Position retained for time specified by commander.
02	Percent	Of friendly forces available to continue mission.
03	Percent	Combat effectiveness of enemy force.

TACTICAL TASK 8.0 DEFEND FROM COMPLEX BATTLE POSITION

B-10. *Complex battle positions* (CBPs) are designed to protect the units within them from detection and attack while denying their seizure and occupation by the enemy. They are not necessarily tied to an avenue of approach. CBPs protect forces while providing sanctuary from which to launch local attacks. The subtasks for defense from a CBP are—

- **8.1 Protect**
  - Employ complex terrain, survivability, and C3D to protect the defending force from destruction.
- **8.2 Degrade**
  - Retain ability to conduct systems warfare actions from protected positions.

TACTICAL TASK 8.0 DEFEND FROM COMPLEX BATTLE POSITION		
No.	**Scale**	**Measure**
01	Yes/No	Position retained for time specified by commander.
02	Percent	Of friendly forces available to continue mission.
03	Yes/No	Able to conduct specified systems warfare missions.

TACTICAL TASK 9.0 ACTIONS ON CONTACT

B-11. *Actions on contact* are designed to ensure OPFOR units retain the initiative and fight under circumstances of their choosing. Actions on contact are also designed to provide the commander with the flexibility to either continue with the planned course of action or rapidly adopt a new course of action more suited to changed conditions. The subtasks for actions on contact are—

- **9.1 Fix**
  - Prevent the enemy from moving any part of his force from a specific location for a specific period of time.
  - Security element(s) making contact fix the enemy.
  - Security element(s) continue to provide early warning of approaching enemy forces and prevent them from gaining further information on the rest of the OPFOR force.

Note. Security element(s) performing a fixing function are then known as fixing element(s). Fixing elements often make use of terrain chokepoints, obstacles, ambushes and other techniques to fix a larger force. When an element that is not a security element makes contact with the enemy, the commander will designate that element as a fixing element.

- **9.2 Assess and Report**
  - Commander makes an assessment of the tactical situation and determines whether or not making contact in this manner and with this enemy constitutes a change in his course of action.
  - Commander reports to the chain of command the form of contact he has made, to include critical details of its composition and his assessment.
- **9.3 Isolate**
  - Maneuver and deploys security element(s) to ensure additional enemy forces do not join the battle unexpectedly.
- **9.4 Maintain Freedom to Maneuver**
  - Make contact with the minimum force necessary to fix the enemy.
  - Make use of C3D and the break contact battle drill to prevent the OPFOR force from becoming decisively engaged.
  - Determine safe maneuver avenues to employ.
  - Freedom to maneuver is also maintained by dominating avenues of approach into the battle zone and determining the location of enemy flanks or exposed areas of weakness.
- **9.5 Execute Course of Action**
  - Contacting unit either continues with its original course of action if deemed appropriate or executes a new one that suits the situation.
  - New course of action given to the unit based on the assessment it provides to its higher command or one chosen by the commander in absence of time or guidance.
  - Unit making contact ensures follow-on units are aware of the contact and deconflict positioning, typically through the use of a standard marking system.

TACTICAL TASK 9.0 ACTIONS ON CONTACT		
No.	**Scale**	**Measure**
01	Yes/No	Unit fixes enemy.
02	Yes/No	Unit leader assesses situation without main body being in contact with the enemy.
03	Time	To report.
04	Yes/No	Unit isolates enemy from assistance.
05	Time	To choose course of action (COA).
06	Time	To execute selected COA.
07	Time	To recommend a COA to the higher commander.
08	Time	To return to previous mission.
09	Percent	Of friendly forces available to continue previous mission.
10	Percent	Combat effectiveness of enemy force that made contact.
11	Percent	Correctness of initial assessment of enemy.

TACTICAL TASK 10.0 SITUATIONAL BREACH

B-12. A *situational breach* is the reduction of and passage through an obstacle encountered in the due course of executing another tactical task. The unit conducting a situational breach may have expected an obstacle or not, but in either case conducts a situational breach with the resources at hand and does not wait for specialized equipment and other support. The subtasks for situational breach are—

- **10.1 Isolate**
  - Maneuver and deploy security element(s) to ensure additional enemy forces do not join the battle unexpectedly. (Security elements may become fixing elements.)
  - Continue to provide early warning.
  - Prevent enemy from gaining further information.
  - Prevent enemy maneuver.
- **10.2 Secure**
  - Unit takes action to ensure enemy defending the obstacle are neutralized.
- **10.3 Penetrate**
  - Clearing element neutralizes the obstacle such that the action element and/or a follow-on force can complete its mission.
- **10.4 Execute Course of Action**
  - Breaching unit continues with its original course of action if deemed appropriate or executes a new one that suits the situation.
  - New course of action given to the unit based on the assessment it provides to its higher command or one chosen by the commander in absence of time or guidance.
  - Breaching unit ensures follow-on units are aware of the obstacle facilitates movement, typically through the use of a standard marking system.

TACTICAL TASK 10.0 SITUATIONAL BREACH		
No.	Scale	Measure
01	Yes/No	Unit isolates breach site from contact.
02	Time	To secure breach site.
03	Time	To penetrate obstacle.
04	Time	To return to previous mission.
05	Percent	Of friendly forces available to continue previous mission.

TACTICAL TASK 11.0 BREAKING CONTACT

B-13. The primary consideration in *breaking contact* is to remove the enemy's ability to place destructive or suppressive fires on the greater portion of the OPFOR force. This is accomplished by fixing the enemy, regaining freedom to maneuver and employing fires, counter-mobility and camouflage, concealment, cover, and deception (C3D). The subtasks for break contact are—

- **11.1 Protect**
  - Take immediate steps to protect the unit from this form of contact.
  - Direct fire: fix, C3D, terrain use.
  - Sensor collection: C3D, terrain use, alternate assembly areas/positions.
  - Emplaced obstacles and chemical, biological, radiological, and nuclear (CBRN): alternate assembly areas/positions.
  - Air, indirect fires, and electronic warfare: C3D, terrain use, alternate assembly areas/positions.
- **11.2 Retain Freedom to Maneuver**
  - Commander reduces his elements in contact to only security element(s).
  - Commander selects one or more routes from his current location that enable his detachment to remain out of contact while permitting him to maneuver in support of his mission.
- **11.3 Assess and Report**
  - Commander reports to the chain of command the form of contact he has made and critical details of its composition and his assessment.
- **11.4 Continue or Change in Course of Action**
  - Commander makes an assessment of the tactical situation to determine whether or not making contact in this manner and with this enemy constitutes a change in the course of action (COA).

TACTICAL TASK 11.0 BREAK CONTACT		
No.	**Scale**	**Measure**
01	Time	To implement appropriate protective measures.
02	Yes/No	Unit leader assesses situation without main body being in contact.
03	Time	To report.
04	Time	To retain/choose COA.
05	Percent	Of friendly forces available to continue.
06	Percent	Correctness of initial assessment of contact.

TACTICAL TASK 12.0 FIXING

B-14. *Fixing* is a tactical task intended to prevent the enemy from moving any part of his force from a specific location for a period of time. The ability to fix the enemy at crucial points is the fundamental way units maintain the freedom to maneuver and retain the initiative. An enemy becomes fixed in one of three basic ways: he cannot physically move, he does not want to move, or he does not think he can move. Suppressive fires, information warfare (INFOWAR) and countermobility are the primary methods by which an enemy is fixed in this way. The subtasks for fixing are—

- **12.1 Prevent Enemy Movement**
  - Physically prevent enemy from moving.
  - Make the enemy believe he cannot move.
  - Make the enemy believe he does not want to move.
- **12.2 Execute Fixing Method or Action**
  - Suppressive fires.
  - INFOWAR.
  - Countermobility.

TACTICAL TASK 12.0 FIXING		
No.	**Scale**	**Measure**
01	Yes/No	Enemy was fixed.
02	Time	To select fixing action/method.
03	Time	To execute fixing action/method.
04	Percent	Of friendly force able to continue mission.

TACTICAL TASK 13.0 TACTICAL MOVEMENT

B-15. *Tactical movement* is the method by which OPFOR units move on the battlefield. It is employed in any situation where enemy contact is possible. It is most often used in offensive operations, to move from attack position to the point of attack. The subtasks for tactical movement are—

- **13.1 Organize**
  - Fighting patrols.
  - Security elements.
  - Security detachment.
  - Main body.
  - Routes, axes, attack zones, firing lines.
- **13.2 Maintain Freedom to Maneuver**
  - Make contact with the minimum force necessary to fix the enemy.
  - Make use of C3D and the break contact battle drill to prevent the moving force from becoming decisively engaged.
  - Security element(s) determine safe maneuver avenues to employ.

TACTICAL TASK 13.0 TACTICAL MOVEMENT		
No.	**Scale**	**Measure**
01	Yes/No	Fighting patrol/security element fixes enemy.
02	Yes/No	Unit leader assesses situation without main body being in contact with the enemy.
03	Time	To report.
04	Time	To choose and move to alternate route(s).
05	Time	To return to previous mission.
06	Percent	Of friendly forces available to continue previous mission.
07	Percent	Combat effectiveness of enemy force that made contact.

TACTICAL TASK 14.0 DISRUPTION

B-16. *Disrupt* is a tactical task intended to upset an enemy's formation or tempo, interrupt the enemy's timetable, cause the enemy to commit his forces prematurely, and/or cause him to attack in piecemeal fashion. The purpose of a disruption force is to significantly degrade the enemy's combat capability and to prevent the enemy from conducting an effective operation. The primary task of the disruption force is to initiate the attack against the enemy's combat system. The subtasks for disruption are—

- **14.1 Destroy or Deceive Enemy Reconnaissance**
- **14.2 Gain and Maintain Reconnaissance Contact with Key Enemy Elements**
- **14.3 Contain the Enemy**
  - Stop, hold, or surround enemy forces.
  - Prevent the enemy from withdrawing any element for use elsewhere.
- **14.4 Destroy the Enemy**
  - Render the enemy combat ineffective and/or damage elements of the enemy's combat system to the point of uselessness.
- **14.5 Exfiltrate**

■ Conduct undetected movement from areas under enemy control by stealth, deception, surprise, or clandestine means.

TACTICAL TASK 14.0 DISRUPTION		
No.	Scale	Measure
01	Yes/No	Enemy reconnaissance able to locate friendly high-value targets (HVTs) destroyed or deceived.
02	Percent	Enemy HVTs identified, tracked, destroyed.
03	Time	Enemy delayed.
04	Yes/No	Enemy forced to deploy to friendly time schedule.
05	Yes/No	Enemy main body contained.
06	Percent	Of friendly forces available to continue mission.
07	Percent	Combat effectiveness of enemy force.

TACTICAL TASK 15.0 INTEGRATED ATTACK

B-17. *Integrated attack* is an offensive action where the OPFOR seeks military decision by destroying the enemy's will and/or ability to continue fighting through the application of combined arms effects. Integrated attack is often employed when the OPFOR enjoys overmatch with respect to its opponent and is able to bring all elements of offensive combat power to bear. It may also be employed against a more sophisticated and capable opponent, if the appropriate window of opportunity is created or available. The subtasks for integrated attack are—

- 15.1 Planning
  - ■ Determine decisive points.
  - ■ Backwards plan from destruction of critical enemy combat service support and command and control (C2) organizations back to the current time.
    - o Destruction of objective.
    - o Maneuver of exploitation force to objective.
    - o Use of assault force to enable exploitation force.
    - o Fixing force isolates decisive points.
    - o Disruption force executes disruption of enemy.
    - o Rehearsals.
    - o Preparation.
    - o Planning.
- 15.2 Preparation
  - ■ Create task organization and C2 of disruption force, fixing force, assault force, exploitation force, reserves, and deception force.
  - ■ Execute deception and disruption.
- 15.3 Rehearsal
- 15.4 Execution
  - ■ Disruption force executes disruption of enemy; focuses on preventing detection of exploitation force.
  - ■ Fixing force(s) maneuver and fire to ensure the decisive point is isolated.
  - ■ Maneuver and deploy security element(s) to ensure additional enemy forces do not join the battle unexpectedly. (Security elements may become fixing forces.)

- Assault force conducts action to set conditions for exploitation force success.
- Exploitation force destroys target enemy or seizes objective.

TACTICAL TASK 15.0 INTEGRATED ATTACK		
No.	Scale	Measure
01	Yes/No	Mission accomplished.
02	Yes/No	Assault forces created correct conditions for exploitation forces' success.
03	Time	To complete mission.
04	Yes/No	Fixing forces isolated decisive points.
05	Yes/No	Disruption forces accomplished mission.
06	Percent	Of friendly forces available to continue previous mission.
07	Percent	Combat effectiveness of enemy force.
08	Percent	Correctness of initial assessment of enemy.

TACTICAL TASK 16.0 DISPERSED ATTACK

B-18. *Dispersed attack* is the primary manner in which the OPFOR conducts offensive action when threatened by a superior enemy and/or when unable to mass or provide integrated C2 to an attack. This is not to say that the dispersed attack cannot or should not be used against peer forces, but as a rule integrated attack will more completely attain objectives in such situations. Dispersed attack relies on INFOWAR and dispersion of forces to permit the OPFOR to conduct tactical offensive actions while overmatched by precision standoff weapons and imagery and signals sensors. The dispersed attack is continuous and comes from multiple directions. It employs multiple means working together in a very interdependent way. The attack can be dispersed in time as well as space. The subtasks for dispersed attack are—

- **16.1 Planning**
  - Determine decisive points.
  - Determine need for window of opportunity and/or multiple exploitation forces.
  - Backwards plan from destruction of key elements of the enemy's combat system back to the current time.
    - Destruction of objective(s).
    - Maneuver of exploitation forces to objective(s).
    - Use of assault force(s) to enable exploitation force.
    - Fixing force(s) isolate decisive points.
    - Disruption force(s) execute disruption of enemy.
    - Rehearsals.
    - Preparation.
    - Planning.
- **16.2 Preparation**
  - Create task organization and C2 of disruption force(s), fixing force(s), assault force(s), exploitation force(s), reserves, and deception force.
  - Execute deception and disruption.
- **16.3 Rehearsal**

- **16.4 Execution**
  - Disruption force(s) execute disruption of enemy.
  - Focus on preventing detection of exploitation forces.
  - Fixing forces maneuver and fire to ensure the decisive point is isolated.
  - Maneuver and deploy security element(s) to ensure additional enemy forces do not join the battle unexpectedly. (Security elements may become fixing elements.)
  - Assault force(s) conduct action to set conditions for exploitation forces' success.
  - Exploitation force(s) destroys target enemy or seize objectives.

TACTICAL TASK 16.0 DISPERSED ATTACK		
No.	**Scale**	**Measure**
01	Yes/No	Mission accomplished.
02	Yes/No	Assault forces created correct conditions for exploitation forces' success.
03	Time	To complete mission.
04	Yes/No	Fixing forces isolated decisive points.
05	Yes/No	Disruption forces accomplished their mission.
06	Percent	Of friendly forces available to continue previous mission.
07	Percent	Combat effectiveness of enemy force.
08	Percent	Correctness of initial assessment of enemy.

TACTICAL TASK 17.0 FIRE AND MANEUVER

B-19. *Fire and maneuver* is the way in which OPFOR small units move while in contact with the enemy. When required to move while in contact with the enemy, the OPFOR commander selects a part of his force to be the support (or firing) element and part to be the action (or moving) element. The support element then directs suppressing fire against any enemy that has the ability to influence the movement of the action element. The action element then moves either to a firing line or to the objective. Once it reaches its new position, it becomes the new support element, and the former support element becomes the new moving element.

Note. The critical aspect of executing fire and maneuver is the commander's selection of the right amount of combat power and resources to assign to each of the elements of his force. If the support element does not have the ability to significantly reduce the effectiveness of the enemy, the action element will be destroyed. If the action element does not have the combat power to take the objective or assume its new role as support element, the mission will fail.

B-20. The subtasks for fire and maneuver are—
- **17.1 Make Contact**
- **17.2 Fix**
  - Prevent the enemy from moving any part of his force from a specific location for a specific period of time.
  - Commander selects a part of his force to be the support (or firing) element and part to be the action (or moving) element.

■ Support element directs suppressing fire against any enemy that has the ability to influence the movement of the action element.

■ Security element(s) continue to provide early warning of approaching enemy forces and prevents them from gaining further information on the rest of the OPFOR force.

Note. A support element that prevents other parts of the enemy force from influencing the movement of the action force is then known as a fixing element. Fixing elements often make use of terrain chokepoints, obstacles, ambushes and other techniques to fix a larger force. When contact is made with an element that is not a support element, the commander will designate that element as a fixing element.

● **17.3 Isolate**

■ Maneuver and deploy security element(s) to ensure additional enemy forces do not join the battle unexpectedly. (Security elements may become fixing elements.)

● **17.4 Maneuver**

■ Action element maneuvers to new position of advantage with respect to the enemy.

■ On order, action element assumes role as new support element or assaults the enemy.

■ If further maneuver is required, continue alternation of fixing the enemy and maneuvering against enemy.

TACTICAL TASK 17.0 FIRE AND MANEUVER		
No.	**Scale**	**Measure**
01	Yes/No	Unit fixes enemy.
02	Yes/No	Unit leader correctly structures his force quickly into support and action elements.
03	Yes/No	Support element suppresses enemy.
04	Yes/No	Security element isolates enemy from assistance.
05	Yes/No	Action element maneuvers to position of advantage.
06	Time	To make each maneuver.
07	Time	To assault and destroy enemy.
08	Percent	Of friendly forces available to continue previous mission.
09	Percent	Combat effectiveness of enemy force that made contact.
10	Percent	Correctness of initial assessment of enemy.

TACTICAL TASK 18.0 ALL-ARMS AIR DEFENSE

B-21. *All-arms air defense* is the simultaneous employment of several arms, in some cases including air defense systems, to achieve an effect against the enemy air threat that will render greater results than the use of air defense assets and systems alone. Thus, all OPFOR units possess some type of an organic air defense capability to differing degrees, depending on the type and size of the unit. The extent to which this capability can be applied is limited only by the commander and staff's knowledge of the enemy air threat, capabilities of their own systems, and their ability to apply that knowledge to come up with innovative solutions. The subtasks for all-arms air defense are—

- **18.1 Planning**
  - Locate or predict enemy airfields; forward arming and refueling points (FARPs); flight routes; drop, landing, and pickup zones (DZ/LZ/PZ); and helicopter firing positions.
  - Determine need for window of opportunity.
  - Backwards plan from destruction of aircraft back to the current time.
    - o Destruction of aircraft.
    - o Detection of aircraft.
    - o Maneuver to firing position and/or placement of obstacles.
    - o Use of C3D and window(s) of opportunity.
    - o Disruption force(s) executes disruption of enemy.
    - o Rehearsals.
    - o Preparation.
    - o Planning.
  - Look for new and adaptive ways of employing existing capabilities (not only air defense systems but also systems not traditionally associated with air defense) to damage and/or destroy enemy aircraft when within range.
  - Identify complex terrain in the vicinity of identified targets and potential cache sites.
  - Identify affiliated forces (such as insurgent groups, groups with ethnic ties to the OPFOR, groups that sympathize with the OPFOR for political reasons, individual sympathizers, terrorist groups, and criminal organizations) that can perform air defense functions.
  - Determine potential means and routes of infiltration and potential sources of supply.
  - Determine the decisive point for aircraft destruction.
    - o On the ground (using indirect fire, WMD, direct action, or precision munitions).
    - o In flight, but before entering the airspace over OPFOR ground maneuver forces (using air defense weapons, directed energy weapons, or direct fire).
    - o In the airspace above OPFOR battle positions (using air defense weapons, other ground force weapons, obstacles, or anti-helicopter mines).
- **18.2 Preparation**
  - All units incorporate the use of their weapons to engage tactical aircraft into their tactics, techniques, and procedures.
  - All units routinely train in techniques for engaging enemy aircraft.
  - All units execute deception and disruption.
- **18.3 Rehearsal**
- **18.4 Execution**
  - All units post air observers.
  - Detect and report the presence of enemy aircraft (on the ground or in the air).
  - Destroy enemy aircraft.
  - Prevent aerial observation.
  - Force the aircraft to expend their munitions before reaching the optimum or effective range.
  - Divert enemy aircraft before reaching their targets.

- Force the enemy to break off and/or discontinue the air attack.
- Mitigate the effectiveness of the enemy air attack.

TACTICAL TASK 18.0 ALL-ARMS AIR DEFENSE		
No.	Scale	Measure
01	Yes/No	Prevented enemy aircraft from interfering with OPFOR missions.
02	Yes/No	Defended the unit from aerial observation and air attack.
03	Percent	Destroyed enemy aircraft.
04	Yes/No	Forced enemy aircraft to expend their munitions before reaching the optimum or effective range.
05	Yes/No	Diverted enemy aircraft before reaching their targets.
06	Yes/No	Forced the enemy to break off and/or discontinue the air attack.
07	Percent	Mitigated the effectiveness of the enemy air attack.
08	Percent	Combat effectiveness of enemy aircraft.

TACTICAL TASK 19.0 ANTILANDING ACTIONS

B-22. *Antilanding actions* are those methods used to prevent landings by airborne or heliborne troops or to destroy enemy landing forces on the ground as soon after landing as possible. Antilanding actions can and will be executed by any force with the capability to affect the aircraft or the landing forces. However, this is a combined arms action that primarily falls to the antilanding reserve (ALR) for execution. The subtasks for antilanding actions are—

- **19.1 Planning**
  - Locate and predict drop and landing zones (DZs or LZs).
  - Determine need for window of opportunity.
  - Backwards plan from destruction of landing forces back to the current time.
    - o Destruction of landing forces.
    - o Detection of landing forces.
    - o Maneuver to firing position and/or placement of obstacles.
    - o Use of C3D and window(s) of opportunity.
    - o Disruption force(s) execute disruption of enemy.
    - o Rehearsals.
    - o Preparation.
    - o Planning.
  - Identify complex terrain in the vicinity of identified targets and potential cache sites.
  - Identify affiliated forces (such as insurgent groups, groups with ethnic ties to the OPFOR, groups that sympathize with the OPFOR for political reasons, individual sympathizers, terrorist groups and criminal organizations) that can perform or support antilanding functions.
  - Determine potential means and routes of infiltration and potential sources of supply.
  - Determine the decisive point for destruction of landing forces.
    - o On the ground, before air transport (using indirect fire, WMD, direct action, or precision munitions).

o En route to or in the vicinity of LZs or DZs (using air defense weapons, directed energy weapons, direct fire, obstacles, or anti-helicopter mines).

o In an LZ or DZ (using indirect fire, WMD, direct fire, direct action, precision munitions, or infantry with antitank weapons).

Note. The OPFOR prefers to prevent landings by airborne or heliborne troops through the destruction of the troop transport aircraft in flight. Failing that, it will take significant actions to destroy landing forces on the ground as soon after landing as possible. Antilanding forces are given their own attack zone to control their actions against landing forces. Such an attack zone may only be activated for the duration of an antilanding action or may be assigned to the ALR permanently. Kill zones are used to control both ground and air defense engagements.

- **19.2 Preparation**
  - Create one or more ALRs.
  - Create task organization and C2 of action element(s), support element(s), security element(s), and deception force.
  - Assign attack zone(s) and kill zone(s).
- **19.3 Rehearsal**
  - The ALR rehearses actions in the vicinity of the LZs or DZs as well as movement between assembly areas, hide positions, and attack positions, and between LZs or DZs.
- **19.4 Execution**
  - Transmit early warning from the main command post to the ALR.
  - ALR moves to positions in the attack zone from which it can engage transport aircraft and destroy landing forces on the ground.
    - o Disruption force(s) execute disruption of the enemy; focus on preventing detection of action element(s).
    - o Security element(s) maneuver and fire to ensure the decisive point is isolated to ensure additional enemy forces do not join the battle unexpectedly. (Security elements may become fixing elements.)
    - o Support element(s) conduct action to set conditions for action elements' success.
    - o Action element(s) destroy targeted enemy.

TACTICAL TASK 19.0 ANTILANDING ACTIONS		
No.	**Scale**	**Measure**
01	Yes/No	Mission accomplished.
02	Yes/No	Support element(s) created correct conditions for action elements' success.
03	Time	To complete mission.
04	Yes/No	Security element(s) isolated decisive points.
05	Yes/No	Disruption force(s) accomplished their mission.
06	Percent	Of friendly forces available to continue previous mission.
07	Percent	Combat effectiveness of enemy force.
08	Percent	Correctness of initial assessment of enemy.

TACTICAL TASK 20.0 SOPHISTICATED AMBUSH

B-23. A *sophisticated ambush* is the linking in time and task of RISTA, attacking forces, and window of opportunity to destroy key enemy systems or cause politically unacceptable casualties. What makes a sophisticated ambush "sophisticated" is not the actual attack means. In fact, the actual ambush is executed by tactical-level forces. What makes it "sophisticated" is the linking of sensor, ambusher, window of opportunity, and a target that affects an enemy center of gravity. This may require sophisticated ambushes to be planned, coordinated, and resourced at the operational level. (See chapter 3, FM 7-100.1.) The subtasks and sub-subtasks for the sophisticated ambush are—

- **20.1 Planning**
  - Choose the target enemy force or system. (In a system's warfare approach, this force or system is typically chosen for its role in the enemy's combat system.)
  - Locate and predict target locations.
  - Determine need for window of opportunity.
  - Backwards plan from destruction of target back to the current time.
    - Destruction of target.
    - Tracking of target.
    - Maneuver to firing position and/or placement of obstacles.
    - Use of C3D and window(s) of opportunity.
    - Disruption force(s) execute disruption of enemy.
    - Rehearsals.
    - Preparation.
    - Planning.
  - Identify complex terrain in the vicinity of identified targets and potential cache sites.
  - Identify affiliated forces (such as insurgent groups, groups with ethnic ties to the OPFOR, groups that sympathize with the OPFOR for political reasons, as well as individual sympathizers, terrorist groups, and criminal organizations) that can participate or assist in the sophisticated ambush.
  - Identify potential means and routes of infiltration and potential sources of supply.
  - Determine the decisive point.
  - Establish attack zone and kill zone(s).

Note. Sophisticated ambushes can be executed by any force with the capability to destroy the target. Forces or elements conducting sophisticated ambushes are given their own attack zone to control their actions. Such an attack zone is only activated for the duration of the action. Kill zones are used to control both ground and air engagements.

- **20.2 Preparation**
  - Create task organization and C2 of action element(s), support element(s), security element(s), disruption force(s), and deception force.
  - Execute deception and disruption.
- **20.3 Rehearsal**
  - Ambushing detachment rehearses actions in the vicinity of the kill zone as well as movement between assembly areas, hide positions, and attack positions.
- **20.4 Execution**
  - *Occupy the Ambush Site 20.4.1*
  - *Isolate the Kill Zone 20.4.1*
    - o Maneuver and deploy security element(s) to ensure additional enemy forces do not join the battle unexpectedly. (Security elements may become fixing elements.)
    - o Security element(s) continue to provide early warning.
    - o Prevent the enemy from gaining further information.
    - o Prevent enemy maneuver.
  - *Contain the Enemy 20.4.2*
    - o Stop, hold, or surround enemy forces.
    - o Prevent the enemy from withdrawing any element for use elsewhere.
  - *Destroy the Enemy 20.4.3*
    - o Render the enemy combat ineffective and/or damage selected element(s) of his combat system to the point of uselessness.
  - *Exfiltrate 20.4.4*
    - o Conduct undetected movement from areas under enemy control by stealth, deception, surprise, or clandestine means.

TACTICAL TASK 20.0 SOPHISTICATED AMBUSH		
No.	**Scale**	**Measure**
01	Yes/No	Unit moves to and occupies ambush site without detection.
02	Yes/No	Unit isolates kill zone from assistance.
03	Time	To execute ambush.
04	Yes/No	Enemy in kill zone during projected time window.
05	Yes/No	Enemy contained in kill zone.
06	Percent	Of friendly forces available to continue previous mission.
07	Percent	Combat effectiveness of enemy force.

TACTICAL TASK 21.0 MANEUVER DEFENSE

B-24. A *maneuver defense* is a type of defensive action designed to achieve tactical decision by skillfully using fires and maneuver to destroy key elements of the enemy's combat system and deny enemy forces their objective, while preserving the friendly force. Within the enemy's combat system, the OPFOR would often target the enemy's C2 or logistics forces rather than his less vulnerable combat and combat support forces. Maneuver defenses cause the enemy to continually lose effectiveness until he can no longer achieve his objectives. They can also economize force in less important areas while the OPFOR moves additional forces onto the most threatened axes. The subtasks for maneuver defense are—

- **21.1 Planning**
  - Plan a succession of defensive lines throughout the area of responsibility (AOR).
  - Plan successive battle positions and repositioning routes throughout the AOR.
  - Identify high-value targets and kill zones.
  - Identify complex terrain in the vicinity of identified targets.
  - Determine decisive points.
  - Backwards plan from destruction of key element(s) of the enemy's combat system back to the current time.
    - o Destruction of objective(s).
    - o Repositioning of forces to expose objective to attack.
    - o Disruption force(s) execute disruption of enemy.
    - o Rehearsals.
    - o Preparation.
    - o Planning.
- **21.2 Preparation**
  - Create task organization and C2 of disruption force, main defense force (contact force and shielding force), reserves, deception force(s), and counterattack force(s.)
  - Execute deception and disruption.
- **21.3 Rehearsal**
- **21.4 Execution**
  - Disruption force executes disruption of enemy; focus on preventing interference with repositioning forces and detection and attack of high-value targets.
  - Contact and shielding forces maneuver and fire to ensure the decisive point is isolated.
  - Counterattack forces destroy key element(s) of the enemy's combat system or seize objective.

TACTICAL TASK 21.0 MANEUVER DEFENSE		
No.	**Scale**	**Measure**
01	Yes/No	Mission accomplished.
02	Yes/No	Disruption force(s) created correct conditions for main defense force (contact and shielding forces) success.
03	Time	To complete mission.
04	Yes/No	Contact and shielding forces isolated decisive points.
05	Percent	Of friendly forces available to continue previous mission.
06	Percent	Combat effectiveness of enemy force.
07	Percent	Correctness of initial assessment of enemy.

TACTICAL TASK 22.0 AREA DEFENSE

B-25. *Area defense* is a type of defensive action designed to achieve a decision by either—

- Forcing the enemy's offensive operations to culminate before he can achieve his objectives or
- Denying the enemy his objectives while preserving combat power until decision can be achieved through strategic operations or operational mission accomplishment.

The area defense does not surrender the initiative to the attacking forces, but takes action to create windows of opportunity that permit forces to attack key elements of the enemy's combat system and cause unacceptable casualties. The subtasks for area defense are—

- **22.1 Planning**
    - Establish locations for complex battle positions within the battle zone.
    - Determine key terrain throughout the battle zone.
    - Develop a counterreconnaissance plan.
    - Locate and predict target locations.
    - Develop an integrated fires plan.
    - Determine decisive points.
    - Establish kill zone(s).
    - Backwards plan from destruction of key elements of the enemy's combat system back to the current time.
        - o Enemy attack culminates before he can achieve his objective or before the protected force is destroyed.
        - o Reconnaissance fires and disruption conduct systems warfare on the enemy.
        - o Disruption force executes disruption of enemy.
        - o Rehearsals.
        - o Preparation.
        - o Planning.
- **22.2 Preparation**
    - Create task organization and C2 of disruption force(s), main defense force, reserves, deception force(s), and counterattack force(s).
    - Designate the protected force (if any).
    - Execute deception and disruption.

- **22.3 Rehearsal**
- **22.4 Execution**
  - Disruption force executes disruption of enemy; focus on preventing interference with repositioning forces and detection/attack of high-value targets.
  - Main defense forces conduct reconnaissance fires and disruption to ensure the enemy culminates his attack before the protected force is destroyed.
  - Counterattack forces destroy key element(s) of the enemy's combat system (often targeting C2 or logistics) or seize objective.

No.	Scale	Measure
\multicolumn{3}{c}{**TACTICAL TASK 22.0 AREA DEFENSE**}		
01	Yes/No	Mission accomplished.
02	Yes/No	Disruption force created correct conditions for main defense force success.
03	Time	To complete mission.
04	Yes/No	Protected force is combat effective.
05	Percent	Of friendly forces available to continue previous mission.
06	Percent	Combat effectiveness of enemy force.
07	Percent	Correctness of initial assessment of enemy.

TACTICAL TASK 23.0 INFORMATION WARFARE

B-26. *Information warfare* (INFOWAR) is defined as specifically planned and integrated actions taken to achieve an information advantage at critical points and times. The goal is to influence an enemy's decisionmaking through his collected and available information, information systems, and information-based processes, while retaining the ability to employ friendly information, information-based processes, and systems. The seven elements or subtasks for INFOWAR are—

- Deception.
- Electronic warfare.
- Perception management.
- Computer warfare.
- Information attack.
- Protection and security measures.
- Physical destruction.

TACTICAL SUBTASK 23.1 DECEPTION

B-27. *Deception* includes measures designed to mislead the enemy by manipulation, distortion, or falsification of information. The OPFOR integrates these deception measures into every tactical action; it does not plan deception measures and activities in an ad hoc manner. A deception plan is always a major portion of the overall INFOWAR plan. The OPFOR formulates its plan of action, overall INFOWAR plan, and deception plan concurrently. It attempts to deceive the enemy concerning the exact strength and composition of its forces, their deployment and orientation, and their intended manner of employment. When successfully conducted, deception activities ensure that the OPFOR achieves tactical surprise, while enhancing force survivability. All deception measures and activities are continuously coordinated with deception plans and operations at higher levels. The sub-subtasks for deception are—

- **23.1.1 Planning**
  - Choose the target enemy force or system. This force or system is typically chosen for its role in the enemy's combat system.
  - Locate and predict target location.
  - Determine need for window of opportunity.
  - Backwards plan from influence of deception target back to the current time.
    - o Deception of target.
    - o Tracking of target.
    - o Maneuver to place deception resources in effective position as necessary.
    - o Use of C3D and window(s) of opportunity.
    - o Disruption force(s) executes disruption of enemy.
    - o Rehearsals.
    - o Preparation.
    - o Planning.
  - Identify complex terrain in the vicinity of identified targets necessary to support deception.
  - Identify potential cache sites required.
  - Identify affiliated forces (such as insurgent groups, groups with ethnic ties to the OPFOR, groups that sympathize with the OPFOR for political reasons, individual sympathizers, terrorist groups, and criminal organizations) that may be required to participate or assist in the deception.
  - Determine potential means and routes of infiltration and potential sources of supply.
  - Choose method(s) of deception that best affect the deception target. This may be a combination of methods and must consider the characteristics of the operational environment and the nature of the larger ongoing operation. Such methods include—
    - o Electronic deception (manipulative, simulative, imitative).
    - o Physical deception (decoys [physical signature], thermal, acoustic).
    - o Influence operations (radio, TV/video, print, Internet).
    - o Military deception (feint, demonstration, ruse).
- **23.1.2 Preparation**
  - Create task organization and C2 of action element(s), support element(s), security element(s), and deception force(s) or element(s).

Note. The battle plan and/or INFOWAR plan may call for the creation of one or more deception forces or elements. This means that nonexistent or partially existing formations attempt to present the illusion of real or larger units. When the INFOWAR plan requires forces to take some action (such as a feint or demonstration), these forces are designated as deception forces or elements in close-hold executive summaries of the plan. Wide-distribution copies of the plan make reference to these forces according to the functional designation given them in the deception story.

  - Execute disruption.
- **23.1.3 Rehearsal**
  - The deception force rehearses actions in a concealed location. This includes any military actions such as movement between assembly areas, hide positions, and attack positions.
- **23.1.4 Execution**
  - Verify deception target.
  - Execute deception actions.
  - Monitor and assess deception effectiveness.

Tactical Subtask 23.1 Deception

No.	Scale	Measure
01	Yes/No	Deception target takes desired action.
02	Yes/No	Deception is not discovered.
03	Time	Target is deceived.

TACTICAL SUBTASK 23.2 ELECTRONIC WARFARE

B-28. *Electronic warfare* (EW) is activities conducted to control or deny the enemy's use of the electromagnetic spectrum, while ensuring its use by the OPFOR. EW capabilities allow an actor to exploit, deceive, degrade, disrupt, damage, or destroy sensors, processors, and C2 nodes. At a minimum, the goal of EW is to control the use of the electromagnetic spectrum at critical locations and times in an OE or to attack a specific system. The OPFOR realizes that it cannot completely deny the enemy's use of the spectrum. Thus, the goal of OPFOR EW is to control (limit or disrupt) his use or selectively deny it at specific locations and times on the battlefield, at the OPFOR's choosing. In this way, the OPFOR intends to challenge the enemy's goal of information dominance.

B-29. For the OPFOR, EW consists of two main activities:

- *Signals reconnaissance* is action taken to detect, identify, locate, and track high-value targets (HVTs) through the use of the electromagnetic spectrum. (Thus, signals reconnaissance is essentially the same as the U.S. task Provide Signals Intelligence on Specified Targets in the Universal Joint Task List. Therefore, it is not covered in detail here in the OPFOR Tactical Task List.)
- *Electronic attack* (EA) supports the disaggregation of enemy forces, primarily through jamming.

The EA-related sub-subtasks for EW are—

- **23.2.1 Planning**
  - Choose the target enemy force(s) and system(s). (In a systems warfare approach, this force or system is typically chosen for its role in the enemy's combat system.)
  - Locate or predict target location.
  - Determine need for window of opportunity.
  - Backwards plan from attack on target back to the current time.
    - Electronic attack (EA) on target.
    - Tracking of target location and activity.
    - Maneuver to place EA resources in effective position as necessary.
    - Use of C3D and window(s) of opportunity.
    - Disruption force(s) execute disruption of enemy.
    - Rehearsals.
    - Preparation.
    - Planning.
  - Identify complex terrain in the vicinity of identified targets necessary to support EA.
  - Identify affiliated forces (such as insurgent groups, groups with ethnic ties to the OPFOR, groups that sympathize with the OPFOR for political reasons, individual sympathizers, terrorist groups, and even criminal organizations) that can participate in support of the EA.
  - Determine potential means and routes of infiltration and potential sources of supply.
  - Choose method(s) of EA that best affect the target.
- **23.2.2 Preparation**
  - Create task organization and C2 of action element(s), support element(s), security element(s), disruption force, and deception force.

- ■ Conduct target location.
- ■ Execute disruption.
- ● **23.2.3 Rehearsal**
  - ■ Action element(s) rehearse actions in a concealed location. This includes any military actions such as movement between assembly areas and hide positions.
- ● **23.2.4 Execution**
  - ■ Verify the target audience (organization or population).
  - ■ Conduct EA.
  - ■ Monitor and assess EA effectiveness.

Tactical Subtask 23.2 Electronic Warfare		
No.	**Scale**	**Measure**
01	Yes/No	EA has desired effect.
02	Yes/No	Action and support elements not discovered.
03	Time	Target is affected.
04	Time	To place EA into effect.
05	Percent	Of assessment of effectiveness that is correct.
06	Percent	Of friendly forces available to continue mission.
07	Percent	Combat effectiveness of enemy force.

TACTICAL SUBTASK 23.3 PERCEPTION MANAGEMENT

B-30. *Perception management* involves measures aimed at creating a perception of truth that best suits OPFOR objectives. It integrates a number of widely differing activities that use a combination of true, false, misleading, or manipulated information. Targeted audiences range from enemy forces, to the local populace, to world popular opinion. The sub-subtasks for perception management are—

- ● **23.3.1 Planning**
  - ■ Choose the target audience.
  - ■ Coordinate required communications media support.
  - ■ Backwards plan from influence of target back to the current time.
    - o Execute perception management actions.
    - o Verify the target audience (organization or population).
    - o Rehearsals.
    - o Preparation.
    - o Planning.
  - ■ Indentify affiliated forces (such as insurgent groups, groups with ethnic ties to the OPFOR or others that sympathize with the OPFOR for political reasons, individual sympathizers, terrorist groups, and criminal organizations) that can participate or assist in perception management functions.
  - ■ Choose the method(s) of perception management that best affect the target audience. This may be a combination of methods and must consider the characteristics of the operational environment and the nature of the larger ongoing operation. Such methods include—
    - o Psychological warfare (PSYWAR).
    - o Direct action.
    - o Public affairs.
    - o Media manipulation (radio, TV/video, print, Internet).

- **23.3.2 Preparation**
  - Create task organization and C2 of action element(s), support element(s), security element(s), disruption force, and deception force.
  - Study the target audience.
  - Execute disruption.
- **23.3.3 Rehearsal**
  - PSYWAR and direct action forces rehearse actions in a concealed location. This includes any military actions such as movement between assembly areas, hide positions, and attack positions.
- **23.3.4 Execution**
  - Verify the target audience (organization or population).
  - Execute perception management actions (PSYWAR, direct action, public affairs, and/or media manipulation).
  - Monitor and assess perception management effectiveness.

Tactical Subtask 23.3 Perception Management		
No.	Scale	Measure
01	Yes/No	Perception management has desired effect.
02	Time	Target is affected.
03	Percent	Of assessment of effectiveness that is correct.

TACTICAL SUBTASK 23.4 COMPUTER WARFARE AND INFORMATION ATTACK

B-31. *Computer warfare* (CW) consists of attacks that focus specifically on the computer systems, networks, and/or nodes. This includes a wide variety of activities, ranging from unauthorized access (hacking) of information systems for intelligence-collection purposes, to the insertion of malicious software (viruses, worms, logic bombs, or Trojan horses). Such attacks concentrate on the denial, disruption, or manipulation of the integrity of the information infrastructure. The OPFOR may attempt to accomplish these activities through the use of agents or third-party individuals with direct access to enemy information systems. It can also continually access and attack systems at great distances via communications links such as the Internet.

B-32. *Information attack* (IA) is the intentional disruption or distortion of information in a manner that supports accomplishment of the mission. Unlike computer warfare attacks that target the information systems, IAs target the information itself. Attacks on the commercial Internet by civilian hackers have demonstrated the vulnerability of cyber and information systems to innovative and flexible penetration, disruption, or distortion techniques.

B-33. The sub-subtasks for CW and IA are—

- **23.4.1 Planning**
  - Choose the target enemy information technology system. (In a systems warfare approach, this system is typically chosen for its role in the enemy's combat system.)
  - Locate or predict target location.
  - Determine need for window of opportunity.
  - Plan backwards from attack on target back to the current time.
    - o Attack on target.
    - o Tracking of target.
    - o Maneuver to place CW and IA resources in effective position as necessary.
    - o Use of C3D and window(s) of opportunity.
    - o Disruption force(s) executes disruption of enemy.

      o Rehearsals.

      o Preparation.

      o Planning.

- Identify complex terrain in the vicinity of identified targets necessary to support CW.
- Identify affiliated forces (such as sympathetic insurgent groups, groups with ethnic ties to the OPFOR, groups that sympathize with the OPFOR for political reasons, individual sympathizers, terrorist groups, and criminal organizations) that can participate in support of CW or IA.
- Identify potential means and routes of infiltration and potential sources of supply.
- Choose the method(s) of CW and IA that best affect the target, such as—
  - o Destructive intrusion.
  - o Manipulative intrusion.
  - o Electromagnetic pulse (EMP).
  - o Physical destruction.
  - o Power spike or denial.
  - o Undetected information acquisition.

- **23.4.2 Preparation**
  - Create task organization and C2 of disruption force(s), action element(s), support element(s), security element(s), and deception force.
  - Execute disruption.

- **23.4.3 Rehearsal**
  - The forces and elements rehearse actions in a concealed location. This includes any military actions such as movement between assembly areas, hide positions, and attack positions.

- **23.4.4 Execution**
  - Verify the target information or information system(s).
  - Execute CW and IA (destructive intrusion, manipulative intrusion, EMP, physical destruction, power spike or denial, denial of service, and/or undetected information acquisition).

Tactical Subtask 23.4 Computer Warfare and Information Attack		
No.	**Scale**	**Measure**
01	Yes/No	CW/IA has desired effect.
02	Yes/No	CW/IA and support elements not discovered.
03	Time	Target is affected.
04	Time	To place CW/IA into effect.
05	Percent	Of assessment of effectiveness that is correct.
06	Percent	Of friendly forces available to continue mission.
07	Percent	Combat effectiveness of enemy force.

TACTICAL SUBTASK 23.5 PROTECTION AND SECURITY MEASURES

B-34. *Protection and security measures* is an element of INFOWAR that encompass a wide range of activities, incorporating the elements of deception and EW. Successfully conducted protection and security measures significantly enhance tactical survivability and preserve combat power. The OPFOR will attempt to exploit the large number, and apparently superior technology, of the enemy's sensors. For example, it employs software at the tactical level that allows it to analyze the enemy's satellite intelligence collection capabilities and warn friendly forces of the risk of detection. The use of signature-reducing and signature-altering devices, along with diligent application of operations security measures, supports deception activities in addition to denying information. At the tactical level, protection and security measures focus primarily on counterreconnaissance (see Tactical Task 6.0), C3D, and information security. The sub-subtasks for protection/security measures are—

- **23.5.1 Planning**
  - Identify friendly information system(s) that are potential targets for attack. (This system is typically chosen for its significant role in current OPFOR operations and its value to enemy plans.)
  - Identify complex terrain in the vicinity of identified targets, which could support enemy computer warfare or information attacks.
  - Backwards plan from execution of protection and security measures to the current time.
    - o Execute information protection and security measures.
    - o Rehearsals.
    - o Preparation.
    - o Planning.
  - Identify affiliated forces (such as sympathetic insurgent groups, groups with ethnic ties to the OPFOR, groups that sympathize with the OPFOR for political reasons, individual sympathizers, terrorist groups, and criminal organizations) that can assist or participate in support of the enemy attack.
  - Determine potential means and routes of enemy infiltration.
  - Identify vulnerabilities with respect to—
    - o Destructive intrusion.
    - o Manipulative intrusion.
    - o EMP.
    - o Physical destruction.
    - o Power spike or denial.
    - o Information theft.
- **23.5.2 Preparation**
  - Create task organization and C2 of information protection and security forces and elements.
  - Execute disruption.
- **23.5.3 Rehearsal**
  - Conduct rehearsals in a concealed location.
- **23.5.4 Execution**
  - Verify information system(s) to be protected.
  - Execute information protection and security measures.
    - o Counterreconnaissance.
    - o C3D measures.
    - o Information security procedures.

- o Physical security procedures.
- o Personnel security procedures.
- o Pre-emptive actions.
- o Deception.
- Monitor and assess effectiveness or protection and security measures.

Tactical Subtask 23.5 Protection and Security Measures		
No.	Scale	Measure
01	Yes/No	Enemy successful.
02	Percent	Of assessment of effectiveness that is correct.
03	Percent	Of friendly forces available to continue mission.
04	Percent	Combat effectiveness of enemy force.

TACTICAL SUBTASK 23.6 PHYSICAL DESTRUCTION

B-35. *Physical destruction* as an element of INFOWAR is those physical measures taken to destroy critical components of the enemy force. C2 nodes and target acquisition sensors are a major part of the fire support plan during physical destruction action. The OPFOR integrates all types of conventional and precision weapon systems to conduct the destructive fires, to include fixed- and rotary-wing aviation, cannon artillery, multiple rocket launchers, and surface-to-surface missiles. It can also utilize other means of destruction, such as explosives delivered by special-purpose forces (SPF), insurgents, terrorists, or other affiliated forces. Priority targets typically include target acquisition sensors, tactical command posts, and major communication and C2 systems. The sub-subtasks for physical destruction are—

- **23.6.1 Planning**
  - Develop a priority target list.
  - Locate or predict target locations.
  - Develop a comprehensive fire support plan.
  - Identify affiliated forces (such as sympathetic insurgent groups, groups with ethnic ties to the OPFOR, groups that sympathize with the OPFOR for political reasons, individual sympathizers, terrorist groups, and criminal organizations) can participate in support of physical destruction.
  - Determine potential means and routes of infiltration.
  - Develop a deception plan.
- **23.6.2 Preparation**
  - Create task organization and C2 of action element(s), support element(s), security element(s), and deception force(s) to execute physical destruction of prioritized target list.
- **23.6.3 Rehearsal**
  - Conduct rehearsals in a concealed location. This includes any military actions such as movement between assembly areas, hide positions, and attack or firing positions.
- **23.6.4 Execution**
  - Verify location, activity, and dispositions of the target list.
  - Execute physical destruction of target enemy assets.
  - Monitor and assess physical destruction effectiveness.

Tactical Subtask 23.6 Physical Destruction		
No.	Scale	Measure
01	Yes/No	Enemy successful.
02	Percent	Of assessment of effectiveness that is correct.
03	Percent	Of friendly forces available to continue mission.
04	Percent	Combat effectiveness of enemy force.

TACTICAL TASK 24.0 INSURGENCY

B-36. *Insurgent forces* are groups that conduct irregular or unconventional warfare within the borders or their country in order to undermine or overthrow a constituted government or civil authority. An insurgent organization may use more than one form of tactics and, based on its strategy, its actions could cut across the entire spectrum of warfare—employing terror, guerrilla, and conventional military tactics to achieve its goals. The subtasks for insurgent forces are—

- **24.1 Planning**
    - Determine decisive points.
    - Backwards plan from destruction of critical enemy systems and organizations back to the current time.
        - Destruction of objective.
        - Maneuver of action element (s) or exploitation force to objective.
        - Use of enabling force(s) or element(s) to create opportunity for the exploitation force or action element(s).
        - Fixing force(s) or element(s) isolate decisive points.
        - Disruption force(s) execute disruption of enemy.
        - Rehearsals.
        - Preparation.
        - Planning.
    - Task-organize insurgent cells to accomplish all functions while being resistant to enemy counterinsurgency or law enforcement actions.
- **24.2 Preparation**
    - Create task organization and C2 for disruption force(s), action element(s), exploitation force, support element(s), security element(s), and deception force(s).
    - Conduct continuous disruption in order to—
        - Destroy or deceive enemy reconnaissance.
        - Gain and maintain reconnaissance contact with key enemy elements.
        - Prevent the enemy from moving without exposure to continuous attack.
        - Damage key elements of the enemy's combat system to the point of uselessness.
        - Prevent the enemy from constructing a reliable sanctuary.
- **24.3 Rehearsal**
    - Rehearse all actions, as practicable, in locations that are not detectable by the enemy.
- **24.4 Execution**
    - Maintain support of the local population through perception management operations.
    - Conduct counterintelligence, information protection and security measures, and force protection to prevent disruption by enemy operations.

- Integrate ethnic, tribal, cultural, and religious characteristics of the operational environment to support insurgent operations and ensure the local populace remains hostile to enemy goals.
- Secure sanctuary and funding from outside the area of influence of the enemy.
- Infiltrate and exfiltrate. (Ensure all movement is undetected through the use of stealth, deception, local population, surprise, or clandestine means.)
- Employ all means necessary:
  o Conventional: assault, raid, reconnaissance attack, and ambush.
  o Unconventional: bombing/improvised explosive device (IED), kidnapping, shelling, WMD, hijacking, and sabotage.
  o Information warfare: deception, perception management, electronic warfare, computer warfare, information attack, protection and security measures, and physical destruction.

TACTICAL TASK 24.0 INSURGENCY		
No.	Scale	Measure
01	Yes/No	Reconnaissance able to locate enemy high-value targets (HVTs) destroyed or deceived.
02	Percent	Enemy HVTs identified, tracked, and destroyed.
03	Time	Enemy delayed.
04	Yes/No	Enemy forced to deploy to friendly time schedule.
05	Yes/No	Mission accomplished.
06	Percent	Of friendly forces available to continue mission.
07	Percent	Combat effectiveness of enemy force.
08	Yes/No	Insurgent sanctuary penetrated.
09	Yes/No	Insurgent funds and supplies disrupted by enemy operations.

Appendix C

Scenario Blueprints

A training scenario blueprint is a pictorial and textual representation of the results of task and countertask analysis. A blueprint is presented as a course of action (COA) sketch with accompanying text. The actions and entities depicted establish the necessary full spectrum training conditions that provide the opportunity to accomplish training objectives.

SCENARIO BLUEPRINT CONCEPT

C-1. The purpose of a scenario blueprint is to serve as a framework of circumstances and situations that will provide the appropriate full spectrum training for leaders and units. Blueprints should not be considered rigid templates and must be modified to accommodate training desired tasks. They are the result of the exercise design process and provide a starting point for battlefield geometry, potential application of the operational variables (PMESII-PT), logical hybrid threat forces, and training conditions. A training scenario blueprint provides an example of the key circumstances, situations, events and actions of a training event with COA sketches and text.

C-2. Blueprints are intended to be used in conjunction with TC 7-101 to fully develop comprehensive full spectrum training events. A scenario blueprint provides a basis to assess the resources required to establish the conditions of the operational environment (OE) needed to adequately challenge the training tasks based on task and countertask analysis. Once the desired training unit tasks are determined, exercise planners must design an opposing force (OPFOR) to conduct the appropriate countertasks. A training venue may or may not be resourced with all the personnel, equipment, or facilities necessary to create the OE conditions required to fully train units on desired tasks. In the cases where the resources identified as necessary to adequately challenge training tasks are not available, the commander and training planners must assess training risk and develop mitigation strategies. Using this TC provides a tool for commanders and trainers to determine how much training risk is being accepted and what alternatives are available.

C-3. The geostrategic setting for the scenario—commonly known as the "road to war"—is created by exercise planners after all relevant conditions are selected in order to provide a logical framework for understanding the training OE. The strategic setting should reflect the unique character of the available training geography and local requirements. The actual or fictitious adversaries, the description of motivation for activities, and other elements that establish the logic of the OE conditions are added as needed once a training scenario that challenges the training tasks is completed. The identity and motivations of the adversary (real or fictitious) provide a context to the scenario that is necessary but secondary to establishing conditions to adequately challenge training tasks.

EXERCISE DESIGN

C-4. As discussed in chapter 1, the exercise design process begins with the training unit commander selecting his training objectives and the operational theme for the training event. The operational theme may be major combat operations (MCO) or irregular warfare (IW) or a combination. The training objectives are broken down into unit and leader tasks to be trained and the commander's assessment of the unit's current training state. An example set of tasks for a heavy brigade combat team (HBCT) conducting offensive operations in a full-spectrum setting might be—

- Conduct an Attack.
- Conduct Security Operations.

- Conduct Lethal and Nonlethal Fire Support.
- Conduct Mobility Operations.
- Conduct Information Operations.
- Conduct Humanitarian and Civic Assistance.
- Protect Critical Assets.

C-5. Exercise planners examine the training tasks and conduct a countertask analysis to determine what is needed to challenge the tasks at the appropriate level. The countertask analysis includes all the elements of the OE that may be necessary to challenge the tasks. A set of countertasks that challenges the tasks in the above example might be—

- Conduct Maneuver Defense.
- Conduct Disruption.
- Conduct Actions on Contact.
- Conduct Counterreconnaissance.
- Prepare Obstacles.
- Conduct Information Warfare (INFOWAR).
- Conduct Insurgent Operations.

C-6. With the task and countertask analysis complete, the exercise planners choose an OE, an OPFOR, and a set of courses of action (COAs) that provides the countertasks as a challenging set of conditions. Chapter 2 provides the tools to properly scale the OPFOR and develop the needed OE conditions to support the countertasks developed. It also provides the step-by-step process to fill out the blueprint framework with the detailed planning and resources needed to conduct the countertasks.

C-7. Typically, the countertasks suggest a COA. There is not one right solution, so long as the solution chosen challenges the things the unit is trying to accomplish. The sources for OPFOR COAs are the TC 7-100 series. Tactical-level COAs are also listed in appendix B of this TC, which contains the OPFOR Tactical Task List, which is the source for countertasks. Continuing this example, the exercise planners see that the selected countertasks support a particular OPFOR COA. Figure C-1 shows an example of the COA sketch and text (COA statement) that go with the OPFOR countertasks listed above.

SCENARIO BLUEPRINT EXAMPLES

C-8. This appendix provides six examples to explain how scenario blueprints are designed and used. The first example, which describes the process in detail, is a continuation of the exercise design example above. The remaining five examples are provided for illustrative purposes. The six examples each individually focus on an emphasized aspect of full spectrum operations. Three of the examples do so within an MCO operational theme and three within an IW operational theme. All six examples are based on an HBCT conducting tasks relevant to the operational theme. Each scenario blueprint provides for an emphasis on training one component of full spectrum operations with the other components present but not the training focus. However, training tasks associated with the non-emphasis components will be included in the design and conditions established that provide the opportunity to train those designated tasks.

MCO BLUEPRINT EXAMPLES

C-9. The following are three examples of scenario blueprints with an MCO operational theme. One example has an offensive emphasis, one a defensive emphasis, and the other a stability operations emphasis for the training unit.

MCO Blueprint Example 1: Offensive Emphasis Blueprint

C-10. For illustrative purposes, this blueprint is based on the example of training unit tasks and OPFOR countertasks in paragraphs C-4 and C-5 above. In this case, the OPFOR chooses to conduct a maneuver defense involving a combination of regular military and insurgent forces. (See figure C-1.)

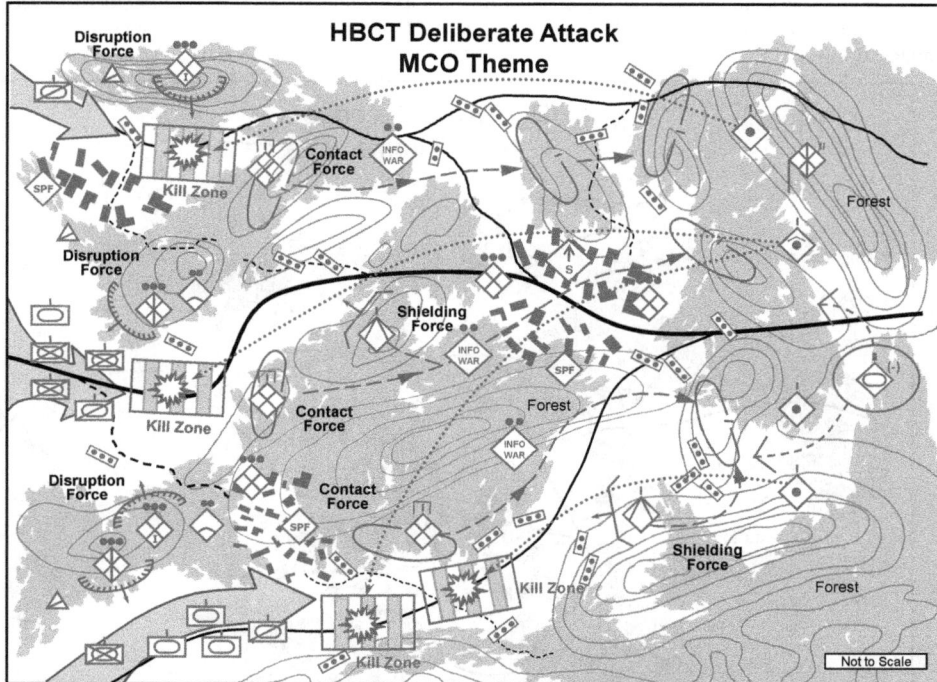

Figure C-1. MCO Blueprint COA sketch (example 1)

C-11. **Course of Action: OPFOR Maneuver Defense.** The OPFOR disrupts command and control (C2) and security forces to deny effective situational understanding and provide freedom of maneuver to the contact force. The disruption force consisting of an infantry-based detachment including special-purpose forces (SPF) teams and affiliated insurgent forces—

- Fixes the reconnaissance squadron.
- Conducts deception, electronic warfare, and perception management.
- Forces the early deployment of the combined arms battalions.
- Destroys intelligence, surveillance, and reconnaissance (ISR) assets.

C-12. The contact force consists of an infantry-based detachment with supporting artillery and information warfare (INFOWAR) assets. It delays the combined arms detachments and forces the HBCT to slow and deploy its fires, sustainment and C2 assets in areas vulnerable to attack by OPFOR fires and the disruption force. The shielding force consists of an antitank-based detachment with supporting artillery and INFOWAR assets. It fixes the two combined arms battalions by conducting attack by fire and permits the contact force to conduct a retrograde to pre-planned battle positions. When this retrograde is complete, the shielding force becomes the new contact force, and the maneuver is repeated until the HBCT's attack is culminated and is vulnerable to counterattack.

C-13. By this point, an initial depiction of the exercise scenario and the sequence of events has emerged. However, the scenario has to be constructed to accommodate training area terrain and constraints. The scenario developer fits the depiction to the terrain and timeline for the training event. The end result is a training event that contains all the components of full spectrum operations in a realistic OE.

MCO Blueprint Example 2: Defensive Emphasis Blueprint

C-14. In this blueprint, the OPFOR chose to use a dispersed attack to overcome some of the U.S. advantages in ISR, close air support, and other stand-off fires. (See figure C-2.) If the training tasks called for the training unit to operate without those enablers, the OPFOR might have chosen to conduct an integrated attack.

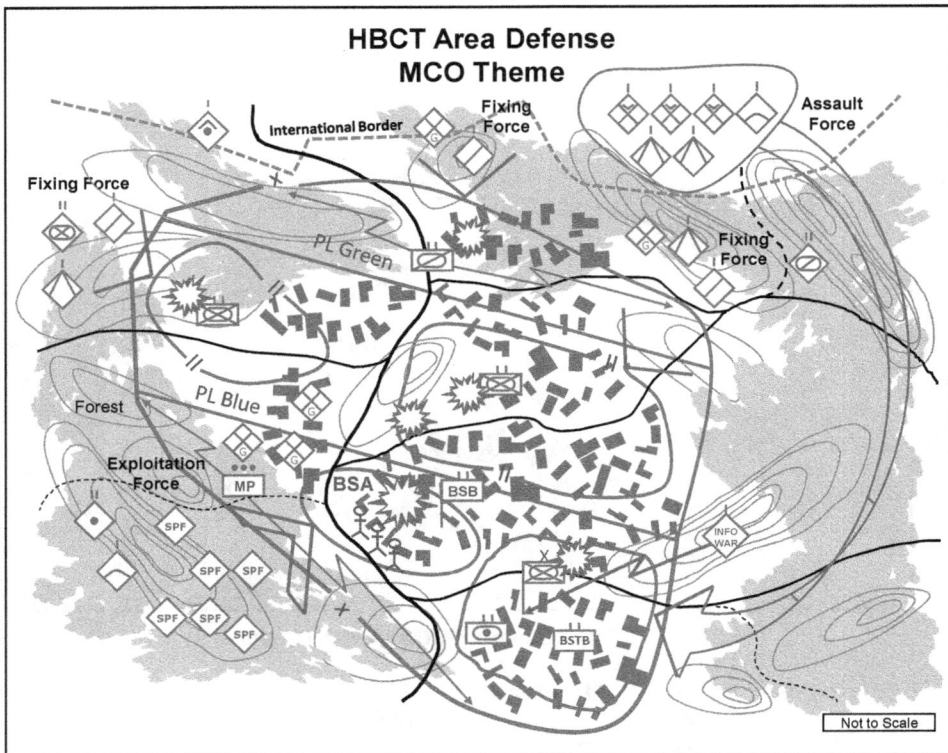

Figure C-2. MCO Blueprint COA sketch (example 2)

C-15. **Course of Action: OPFOR Dispersed Attack.** The OPFOR disrupts C2 and security forces to prevent effective response to other actions and deny effective situational understanding. The disruption force consisting of a reconnaissance battalion, two antitank batteries, an INFOWAR unit, guerrillas, and a supporting rocket launcher battery—

- Fixes the reconnaissance squadron.
- Conducts deception, electronic warfare, and perception management.
- Blocks quick reaction force (QRF) and reserve routes.
- Destroys ISR assets.

C-16. The OPFOR fixes the two combined arms battalions by conducting attacks with three combined arms detachments. The mission of the fixing force is to prevent either combined arms battalion from repositioning significant combat power to protect the HBCT's C2 and sustainment assets from attack. The OPFOR conducts an air assault to destroy HBCT C2 and fires assets in order to permit effective action by the exploitation force. The air assault consists of a battalion-size infantry and antitank detachment augmented by INFOWAR elements. The OPFOR destroys the HBCT's sustainment capability by attacking the brigade support area (BSA) with an exploitation force consisting of six SPF teams, an artillery battalion, an air defense battery, and affiliated guerrilla forces.

MCO Blueprint Example 3: Stability Operations Emphasis Blueprint

C-17. In this blueprint, none of the countertasks chosen include conduct of combat operations by conventional, regular military forces. Therefore, the OPFOR COA focuses on guerrilla operations (see figure C-3).

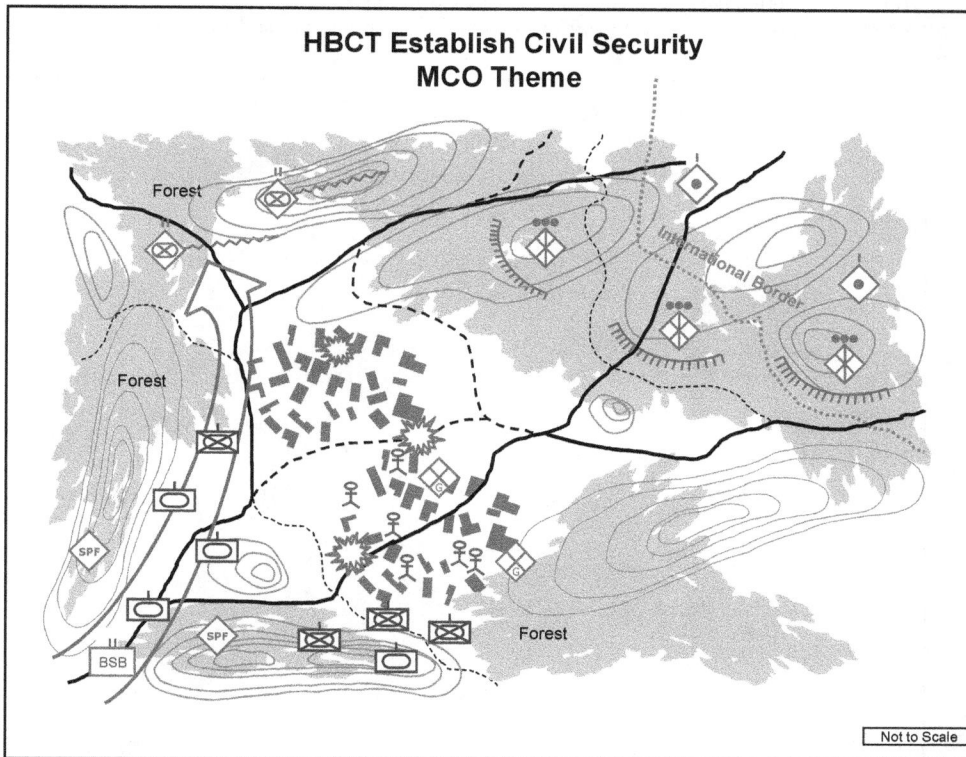

Figure C-3. MCO Blueprint COA sketch (example 3)

C-18. **Course of Action: OPFOR Guerrilla Operations.** The OPFOR disrupts C2 and security forces to deny effective situational understanding and provide freedom of maneuver to the guerrilla force. The disruption force, including guerrilla elements and SPF teams—

- Fixes the reconnaissance squadron (not shown).
- Conducts deception, electronic warfare, and perception management.
- Prevents effective sustainment.
- Prevents the creation of stable civil functions.

C-19. OPFOR conventional force remnants occupy defensive positions or move toward sanctuary—international border or rugged terrain. The conventional force near the international border is prepared to provide aid to guerrilla elements as needed.

IW BLUEPRINT EXAMPLES

C-20. The following are three examples of scenario blueprints with an IW operational theme. (See figures C-4 through C-6.) One example has an offensive emphasis, one a defensive emphasis, and one a stability operations emphasis for the training unit.

IW Blueprint Example 1: Offensive Emphasis Blueprint

C-21. In this blueprint, the countertasks required are executed primarily by regular military forces conducting an area defense, with affiliated guerrilla elements acting as part of the disruption force. (See figure C-4.)

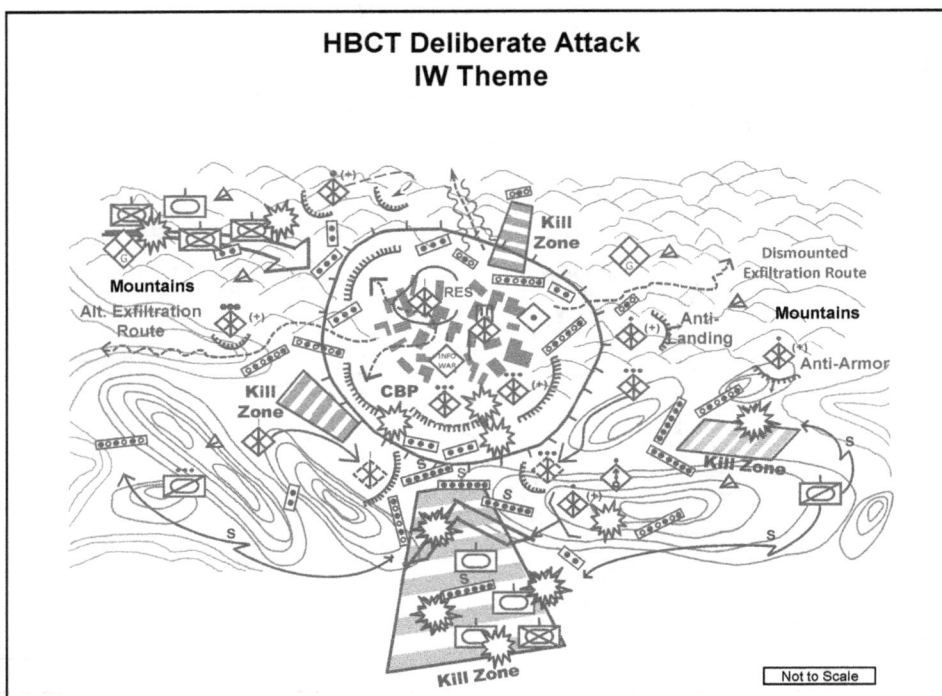

Figure C-4. IW Blueprint COA sketch (example 1)

C-22. **Course of Action: OPFOR Area Defense.** The OPFOR disrupts C2 and security forces to deny effective situational understanding and provide freedom of maneuver to the main defense force. The disruption force outside the complex battle position (CBP) of the main defense force—

- Fixes the reconnaissance squadron (only part of which is shown in figure C-4).
- Conducts deception, electronic warfare, and perception management.
- Forces the early deployment of the combined arms battalions; and destroys ISR assets.

C-23. The main defense force consists of an infantry-based detachment with supporting engineer and air defense assets. It defends from a CBP and protects OPFOR C2, INFOWAR, fires, and sustainment from enemy attack.

C-24. The OPFOR reserve blocks the enemy shaping force and permits freedom of maneuver to the counterattack and main defense forces. The counterattack force blocks the decisive force and permits the protected force (C2, INFOWAR, fires, and sustainment assets) to destroy the HBCT's sustainment and C2 assets and then exfiltrate to remain viable for future battles.

IW Blueprint Example 2: Defensive Emphasis Blueprint

C-25. In this blueprint, the countertasks are executed by guerilla forces attacking a perimeter defense. (See figure C-5.)

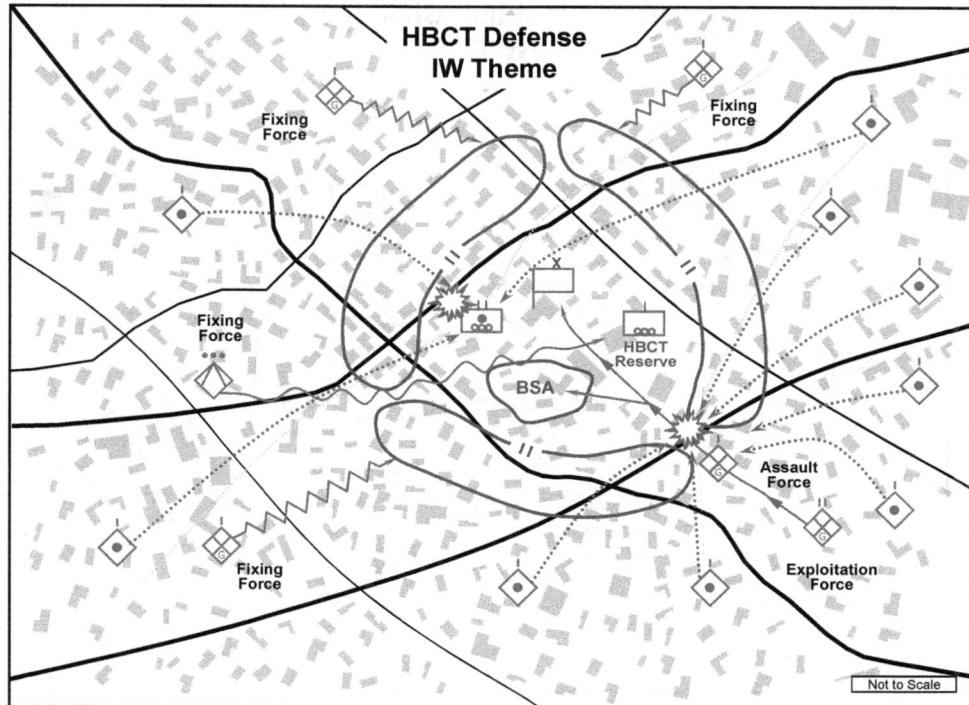

Figure C-5. IW Blueprint COA sketch (example 2)

C-26. **Course of Action: OPFOR Integrated Attack.** The OPFOR disrupts C2 and security forces to prevent effective response to other actions and deny effective situational understanding. The disruption force (not shown)—

- Fixes the reconnaissance squadron.
- Conducts deception, electronic warfare, and perception management.
- Blocks reserve routes.
- Destroys ISR assets.

C-27. The OPFOR fixes the three combined arms battalions by conducting attacks with multiple guerilla elements with supporting fires and antitank assets. The mission of the fixing force is to prevent any of the combined arms battalions from repositioning significant combat power to protect the HBCT's C2 and sustainment assets from attack. The OPFOR conducts an assault with a guerilla element to destroy HBCT C2 and fires assets, to permit effective action by the exploitation force. The OPFOR destroys the HBCT's sustainment capability by attacking the BSA with an exploitation force consisting of guerilla forces.

IW Blueprint Example 3: Stability Operations Emphasis Blueprint

C-28. In this blueprint, the countertasks required are those that oppose stability action. Some of these countertasks will be executed by noncombatant actors opposed to creation of a stable environment due to political, ethnic, or religious motivations. (See figure C-6.)

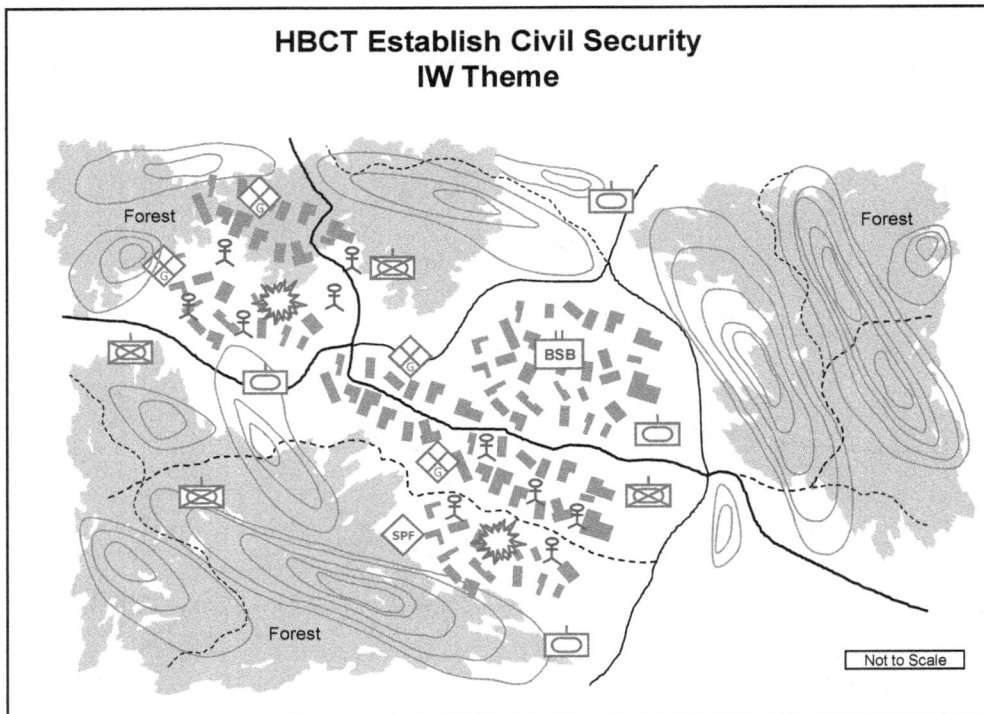

Figure C-6. IW Blueprint COA sketch (example 3)

C-29. **Course of Action: OPFOR Guerrilla Operations.** The OPFOR disrupts C2 and security forces to deny effective situational understanding and provide freedom of maneuver to the guerrilla force. The disruption force fixes the reconnaissance squadron (not shown); conducts deception, electronic warfare, and perception management; prevents effective sustainment; and prevents the creation of stable civil functions.

Glossary

AA	avenue of approach
AAR	after-action review
abn	airborne
ACV	armored command vehicle
AD	air defense
AFS	administrative force structure
AKO	Army Knowledge Online
ALR	antilanding reserve
amphib	amphibious
AO	area of operations
APC	armored personnel carrier
AR	Army regulation
ARFOR	Army forces
ART	Army tactical task
AT	antitank
AUTL	Army Universal Task List
BCT	brigade combat team
BCTP	Battle Command Training Program
BMCT	beginning of morning civil twilight
BMNT	beginning of morning nautical twilight
BSA	brigade support area
BTG	brigade tactical group
C	Celsius
C2	command and control
C3D	camouflage, concealment, cover, and deception
C4I	command, control, communications, computers, and intelligence
CATS	combined arms training strategy
CBP	complex battle position
CBRN	chemical, biological, radiological, and nuclear
cdr	commander
CG	commanding general
cmd	command
COA	course of action
COE	Contemporary Operational Environment
COG	commander, operations group

COMINT	communications intelligence
CPPCG	United Nations Convention on the Prevention and Punishment of the Crime of Genocide
CPX	command post exercise
CR	counterreconnaissance
CTC	combat training center
CW	computer warfare
DAL	defended asset list
DZ	drop zone
EA	electronic attack
EECT	end of evening civil twilight
EENT	end of evening nautical twilight
ELINT	electronic intelligence
EMP	electromagnetic pulse
EW	electronic warfare
EXCON	exercise control
EXROE	exercise rules of engagement
F	Fahrenheit
FARP	forward arming and refueling point
FISINT	foreign instrumentation signals intelligence
FM	field manual
FRAGO	fragmentary order
FSV	fire support vehicle
GPS	global positioning system
HACV	heavy armored combat vehicle
HI	heat index
HQDA	Headquarters, Department of the Army
HUMINT	human intelligence
HVT	high-value target
IA	information attack
IED	improvised explosive device
IFSV	infantry fire support vehicle
IFV	infantry fighting vehicle
IMINT	imagery intelligence
INFOWAR	information warfare
IR	Infrared
ISR	intelligence, surveillance, and reconnaissance
IW	irregular warfare
JFC	joint force commander
JOA	joint operations area
JP	joint publication

JTIDS	joint tactical information distribution system
LOS	line of sight
L-V-C-G	live, virtual, constructive, and gaming
LZ	landing zone
m	Meters
MC	mobility corridor
MCO	major combat operations
MCTC	maneuver combat training center
MEDEVAC	medical evacuation
METL	mission-essential task list
mph	miles per hour
MRX	mission rehearsal exercise
Mt	Mount
N	North
NGO	nongovernmental organization
OB	order of battle
OE	operational environment
OEA	operational environment assessment
OPFOR	opposing force
OPORD	operation order
ops	Operations
OPTEMPO	operational tempo
OSINT	open-source intelligence
P	partially trained
PL	phase line
PMESII-PT	political, military, economic, social, information, infrastructure, physical environment, and time (*see* also PMESII-PT under terms)
POL	petroleum, oil, and lubricants
psnl	Personnel
PSO	private security organization
PSYWAR	psychological warfare
PZ	pickup zone
QRF	quick reaction force
recon	reconnaissance
RISTA	reconnaissance, intelligence, surveillance, and target acquisition
SATCOM	satellite communications
SBP	simple battle position
SIGINT	signals intelligence
SOP	standing operating procedures
SPF	special-purpose forces
STARTEX	start of exercise

STRAC	Standards in Training Commission
T	trained
TC	training circular
tech	technology
TMD	theater missile defense
TOE	table of organization and equipment
TRADOC	Training and Doctrine Command
TRISA	TRADOC G-2 Intelligence Support Activity
TTP	tactics, techniques, and procedures
U	untrained
U.S.	United States
UAV	unmanned aerial vehicle
UDHR	United Nations Universal Declaration of Human Rights
UHF	ultrahigh frequency
UJTL	Universal Joint Task List
UNECE	United Nations Economic Commission for Europe
veh	vehicle
VHF	very high frequency
WARNO	warning order
WBGT	wet bulb globe temperature
WEG	Worldwide Equipment Guide
WFF	warfighting function
WMD	weapons of mass destruction

SECTION II – TERMS

operational environment

A composite of the conditions, circumstances, and influences that affect the employment of capabilities and bear on the decisions of the commander.

PMESII-PT

A memory aid for the operational variables used to describe an operational environment: political, military, economic, social, information, infrastructure, physical environment, and time.

Contemporary Operational Environment

The collective set of conditions, derived from a composite of actual worldwide conditions, that pose realistic challenges for training, leader development, and capabilities development for Army forces and their joint, intergovernmental, interagency and multinational partners.

References

Department of the Army Forms

The DA Form is available on the Army Publishing Directorate web site (www.apd.army.mil).

DA Form 2028, *Recommended Changes to Publications and Blank Forms.*

Documents Needed

These documents must be available to the intended users of this publication.

FM 1-02. *Operational Terms and Graphics.* 21 September 2004.

FM 7-100.1, *Opposing Force Operations.* 27 December 2004.

FM 7-100.4, *Opposing Force Organization Guide.* 3 May 2007. Associated online organizational directories, volumes I-IV, available on TRADOC G2-TRISA Website at https://www.us.army.mil/suite/files/19296289 (AKO access required). Associated *Worldwide Equipment Guide*, volumes 1-3, available on TRADOC G2-TRISA Website at https://www.us.army.mil/suite/files/14751393 (AKO access required).

JP 1-02. *Department of Defense Dictionary of Military and Associated Terms.* Available online: http://www.dtic.mil/doctrine/jel/doddict/

TC 7-100. *Hybrid Threat.* 26 November 2010.

Readings Recommended

These sources contain relevant supplemental information.

AR 15-6, *Procedures for Investigating Officers and Boards of Officers.* 2 October 2006.

ATTP 3-34.80, *Geospatial Engineering.* 29 July 2010.

FM 2-0, *Intelligence.* 23 March 2010.

FM 2-01.3, *Intelligence Preparation of the Battlefield/Battlespace {MCRP 2-3A}.* 15 October 2009.

FM 3-0, *Operations.* 27 February 2008.

FM 3-07, *Stability Operations.* 6 October 2008.

FM 5-0, *The Operations Process.* 26 March 2010.

FM 7-0, *Training for Full Spectrum Operations.* 12 December 2008.

FM 7-15, *The Army Universal Task List.* 27 February 2009.

JP 2-0, *Joint Intelligence.* 22 June 2007.

JP 2-03, *Geospatial Intelligence Support to Joint Operations.* 22 March 2007.

JP 2-01.3, *Joint Intelligence Preparation of the Operational Environment.* 16 June 2009.

JP 3-0, *Joint Operations.* 17 September 2006.

JP 3-05, *Doctrine for Joint Special Operations.* 17 December 2003.

JP 3-13, *Information Operations.* 13 February 2006.

JP 3-15, *Barriers, Obstacles, and Mine Warfare for Joint Operations.* 26 April 2007.

JP 1-02, *Department of Defense Dictionary of Military and Associated Terms.* 12 April 2001.
TC 2-33.4, *Intelligence Analysis.* 1 July 2009.

This page intentionally left blank.

Index

Entries are by paragraph number unless page (p.) or pages (pp.) is specified.

Entries are by paragraph number unless page (p.) or pages (pp.) is specified.

By order of the Secretary of the Army:

GEORGE W. CASEY, JR.
General, United States Army
Chief of Staff

Official:

JOYCE E. MORROW
Administrative Assistant to
Secretary of the Army
1030802

DISTRIBUTION:

Active Army, Army National Guard, and United States Army Reserve: Not to be distributed; electronic media only.

www.ingramcontent.com/pod-product-compliance
Lightning Source LLC
Chambersburg PA
CBHW080206300326
41934CB00038B/3386